Faraway Bridges

Trevor Barry

Order this book online at www.trafford.com
or email orders@trafford.com

Most Trafford titles are also available at major online book retailers.

Cover photograph shows Somali Tribesmen drawing
water for their camels from a well in the Northern
Province of Kenya.

Print information available on the last page.

ISBN: 978-1-4120-2430-3 (sc)

Trafford rev. 05/19/2023

 www.trafford.com

North America & international
toll-free: 844-688-6899 (USA & Canada)
fax: 812 355 4082

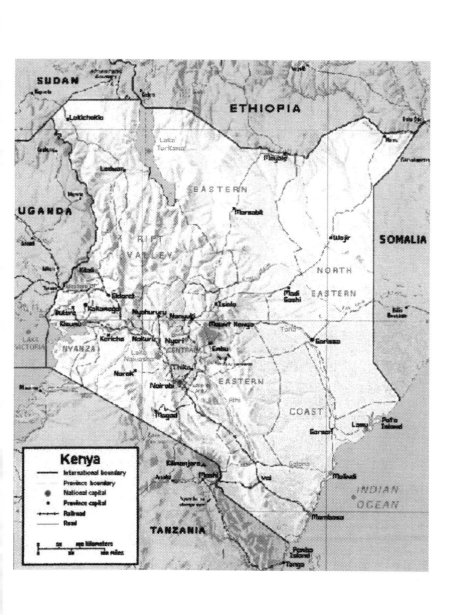

CHAPTER 1.
THE DARK CONTINENT

To those of us who have been lucky enough to have first arrived in East Africa by ship, in the days when this was the normal method of long distance travel, there is nothing quite as exciting, when encountered for the first time, as the strange sights and smells of Africa. So at least it seemed to us who arrived at Mombasa on a hot and sunny day in the month of March 1949. I can still remember the smells of Port Said and Aden where we stopped on our way, a mixture of crude oil and eastern spices.

We experienced the strangeness of these bustling ports with their magicians called "gulli gulli" men, (in whose presence we were advised to keep our hands in our pockets if we did not wish to lose our loose change!) These conjurors were really fantastic sleight of hand merchants and provided excellent entertainment producing chickens and other items with great speed and dexterity, but when they asked for money to work with it had an ability to mysteriously disappear after one or two tricks!

The sea around the ship when we anchored in Port Said and Aden swarmed with masses of small boats filled with persistent salesmen who sent up their goods on baskets pulled up on ropes. These were thrown onto the boat decks and hauled in by the prospective buyer. After the obligatory haggling the basket was then returned with the money when a deal was successfully concluded.

All very different and exciting to persons who had never seen this type of thing before. The articles on sale were mainly clothing goods, rugs, ivory carvings and leather items and on the whole I believe they were of good quality and fairly cheap. Other boats contained young men who called for coins to be thrown into the sea near to them and when the coins landed they dived in after them and in most cases returned to the surface with the coin held in their hands, teeth or between their toes.

When we went ashore and ventured into the shopping bazaars we were immediately surrounded by Arabs of all shapes and sizes selling anything from pornographic pictures to the available ladies of the area, and I think most of us were quite pleased to return to the safety of the ship.

To reach Mombasa we had come down the Suez Canal with its bleak desert on each side and the terrible dry heat of the Red Sea. This was before the days of sophisticated air conditioning and the only air conditioning available on the ship was by blowers. These succeeded only in moving the hot air around the cabins and lounges and provided little relief to the passengers.

Many of the passengers, in fact, abandoned their cabins at night and slept on the deck, where there was at least some small respite from the relentless heat of the day, so it was quite a relief to many of us to finally reach our port of destination.

My fellow travellers were, in the main, a mixture of old hands returning to East Africa, wives going out to join their husbands and a collection of young men, like myself, recruits to the British Colonial Service.

Our transport was an old passenger ship, which had only recently been refitted after use as a troop carrier and was by no means a luxury liner. The crew was friendly and I suppose it would have been described as a "happy" ship.

Shipboard romances flourished as they do on these occasions and I am sure that some embarrassing moments must have occurred at a later date, when returned wives, reunited with their husbands, came face to face with the romantic liaisons of the voyage.

Mombasa was then the major port of the British Colony and Protectorate of Kenya, a thriving town where a great many of the liners heading for South Africa and India stopped off for fuel and passengers.

Shortly after the ship had tied up, the Immigration Officers came on board and we went through the usual formalities and those who were to become civil servants were directed to the Government Coast Agent who gave us our final destinations together with the necessary rail warrants.

At this stage a shouting mass of African porters arrived on board and carried our cabin luggage ashore. This was my first introduction to the African labour with which I was to work for many years. I found it interesting to see cabin trunks, which had required the lifting efforts of two white porters and a trolley to bring aboard, being carried out on the back of one hefty African porter!

So I set foot on African soil for the first time in the steaming heat of a day in Mombasa, a town with what had then a mixed population of Africans, Arabs, Indians and white men. During the voyage I had met and teamed up with four fellow travellers that were destined, like myself, to work as professional officers in the Public Works Department. As we were to find out later it was the normal procedure for new arrivals, to be posted to the Nairobi Head Office of the Public Works Department, (later to be re-named the Ministry of Works).

The four of us, two Irishmen and two Englishmen, spent the rest of that first day in the city of Mombasa exploring the fascinating Old Port with its narrow winding streets full of people of all nations and colours.

That same evening found us on our way to the Railway Station and embarked on the overnight train to the capital city of Nairobi.

The rail journey from Mombasa to Nairobi, in those days and I believe, even today, was an overnight trip on a narrow gauge railway that had been built with the help of imported Indian labour in the early days of Kenya's development.

It was at the time a remarkable engineering feat, involving as it did rising from sea level at Mombasa to the thorn bush plains at an altitude of some three thousand feet in some thirty miles and eventually reaching Nairobi at an altitude of around four thousand five hundred feet over a distance of about three hundred miles.

The great difficulties and dangers, which were encountered in this construction work, have been well recorded in several books of the times. I think most people will have read the gory details of the man-eating lions that attacked and killed many labourers during the construction. Malaria and many other tropical diseases, which medical science had not learned how to control in those days, also took a heavy toll of lives during the project.

As the train rattled along and before darkness fell, we were able to see behind us the long length of the train winding up the hills away from the coastal belt. At times the curves were so sharp that we could see the tail of the train below us on the hillside. The narrow gauge made the journey a fairly rocky one as the train gathered speed on the long more level stretches and the carriages swayed from side to side. The carriages were equipped with comfortable berths, but I slept only fitfully due to the sideways movement of the carriages and the hubbub, which arose at each of the many of the several stops during the night. An unusual experience to those unaccustomed to the cheerful noisiness of Africans en masse.

The early dawn in Africa is always a wonderful time of day with the clear air and coolness that comes with the rising of the sun. To us it was enhanced by the by the sight of large herds of antelope and buffalo moving around the open plains, our first sight of the animals that we would become so accustomed to seeing in the course of our time in Kenya.

As we drew into the outskirts of Nairobi, we were able to see the urban populace on its way to work. Lorries, buses and cars roared down the road beside the train, driven with the gay abandon of African drivers, who, as we later realised, appear to have little conception of the awful accidents that could and often did, result from their reckless driving style.

Nairobi had, in those days, many unguarded rail level crossings and it was unfortunate that on one such crossing our train became involved in collision with a lorry, the driver of which choose to ignore the whistle of the oncoming train and tried to beat it across the level crossing. Several passengers in the lorry were injured and the train was delayed for quite some time while two smartly dressed police officers sorted out the accident. It was a rather shattering experience for us at the time, but, unfortunately, one to which we became accustomed after a few years in Africa.

Everywhere that I have been in Africa, local drivers appear to have a tremendous faith in the power of the brakes and horns of their vehicles. Their faith, unfortunately, does not take into account the general rather poor ability of their garage mechanics. African drivers tend to take chances, which would scare the living daylights out of most white men, and the rate of accidents in many African countries reflects this situation.

We were met at the Station by one of the senior expatriate engineers of the Public Works Department and driven to what was to become for the four of us our home base for many years. This was an old Army barracks, which had been taken over as a transit house for expatriates. It was in reality, transitory only for married expatriates, as due to the shortage of Government housing, it was nearly impossible for bachelors to obtain alternative accommodation.

Thika Roadhouse, as it was called, was, in fact, a very happy place for many of us to live in, managed as it was by a fat and cheerful Englishman with a small and constantly harassed Cockney as his Assistant. Since we were nearly all relatively recently arrived in Kenya and were all Government employees, it became practically a social club and provided an easy way to make friends in what otherwise could have been a rather lonely existence.

The Roadhouse always kept some rooms available for bachelors like myself who were often away "in the bush" for several weeks or months at a time and we could be sure of a warm welcome when we returned to civilisation. Among those who became the longer term residents were, at this stage, four Irishmen, all working in the Public Works Department so, I suppose, it was inevitable that, when late night parties took place, the Irish always appeared to be heavily involved.

The day following such a party, the unfortunate Manager often had to deal with complaints from those residents who had suffered from the noise of our celebrations of the previous night. At lunchtime on that day, the Irish contingent would be lectured by the Manager on our bad behaviour in order to mollify the upset residents. We took this in good spirit since, to tell the truth, the Manager himself and his Assistant were frequently involved in these parties.

Many of these parties related to sending someone off on home leave (which occurred on average every three years) and I must say that I often pitied these poor unfortunates since, by what had by now become Roadhouse tradition, they were not allowed to go to bed the night before they left. At this time Government had started sending people home by air, and so these unfortunate people were "poured" on to the plane in a state of semi-intoxication which must have given them, to say the least, a rough journey home.

CHAPTER 2.
DOWN TO WORK

When the four of us finally reported to Headquarters of the Public Works Department, we were posted to different Branches, largely according to our special engineering interests.

I went to the Roads Branch to begin a career in road engineering, a branch of Civil Engineering in which I was to specialise for a great deal of my working career. It was to be expected that as a junior engineer I would receive most of the mundane jobs in road engineering and so I found myself during those first few weeks computing earthworks on a new road design. This was a tiresome chore before the days of modern computers.

Eventually, however, I completed this particular part of this project and was sent out in to the field to assist in the survey and setting out of the line for a new road that was proposed to be constructed from south of Nairobi to the Tanganyika border at a place called Namanaga.

My "boss" for this project was an old Africa hand who I will call Anderson for the purposes of this book. Anderson was a surveyor of the old school who had spent many years of his life in the bush. He sported a genuine wide brimmed bush hat and wore long shorts with buttoned up extensions that could be turned down and pushed in to your stockings. This combined with canvas knee length "mosquito" boots was his method of preventing mosquito attacks at night. I have never seen these fascinating garments on anyone since and they must, I presume, have been a relic of the old days in India, where he had spent a considerable part of his working life. No one could have had a better tutor in his field and he taught me more about surveying from first principles than I could ever have learnt elsewhere. He was also a fascinating raconteur and kept me well entertained in the evening by the campfire with his stories about the early days in Kenya.

We were surveying through an area nominated as a Game Park and which was heavily populated with game of all kinds. The nomadic Masai who lived in harmony with the animals of their country traditionally owned this land. For the first few weeks we lived in tents and our days were spent reconnoitring possible lines for the new road. Since, at this stage, the Ordinance Survey of Kenya was incomplete, we had to use star sights and compasses to set our proposed routes and I found this most interesting work. It entailed going back to basic surveying of a type which was no longer required in more developed countries.

For this preliminary work we used very accurate aneroid barometers to measure heights and the mileometer of our old Bedford truck to measure distances. These old Bedford trucks were extremely tough vehicles, which were much in demand for bush work before the days of the Land Rover. They had wooden bodies with two rows of seats at the back and in lieu of windows they had side curtains of canvas, which could be lowered when it rained.

Unfortunately these vehicles also had very rigid springing with virtually no shock absorbers and this meant a very uncomfortable ride, especially since, in this type of work, they had to be used like a miniature bulldozer in the bush, breaking down small scrub and thorn trees as we followed compass line surveys which required keeping to as straight a line as possible.

Broken springs and punctured tires were common and repairs to these had to be carried in the field by the driver with the assistance of the survey staff, a tough and dirty job which was carried out with great good humour and ingenuity considering the heat and practical difficulties of the location. On occasions when no spare tyre was available due to a previous puncture with the tube a write off, we returned to camp with a tyre packed full of grass!

Although we were daily surrounded by game of all kinds and had to enter, on foot, dongas covered in a thick growth of trees and shrubs in order to measure depths and examine possible bridge site foundations, we had surprisingly few problems with game during this time. I recall that we disturbed at least two leopards in these dried up watercourses, but they left hurriedly and of course lions are too lazy to give trouble during the heat of the day unless you really annoy them. Elephant herds were common but they were generally content to give our noisy Bedford a wide berth, though sometimes we would get a few mock charges to warn us to keep our distance.

The Game Department had loaned us a Game Scout, armed with a .303 rifle, for the duration of the survey through the Game Reserve. It was his duty to ensure that we received no problems from the animal population and he certainly did this very successfully. He accompanied us on all our surveys and I am glad to say that he never had to use his weapon on our behalf. His English was limited to cheerful "Okays" and his gun handling tended to be of the happy-go-lucky variety so that, on occasion, I felt that we were more in danger from his weapon than the big game!

My grasp of Swahili, of necessity, improved rapidly and I was soon able to hold conversations with him and the other survey staff (who had no English at all) and in the end I learned a lot about the wild life of the area from them all.

As it transpired, during the whole duration of the initial survey and subsequent setting out of the road, I can only recall two occasions when I personally had problems with the animal population. On the first occasion Anderson had been called back to Nairobi for some reason and I was myself driving the old Bedford across the plains following as usual a compass line when one front wheel of the vehicle crashed into an old ant bear hole. This was quite a common experience for us, as these holes were frequent and difficult to see in the long grass, particularly after the rainy season when grass and shrub growth was high.

Unfortunately an old wart hog that occupied this

particular hole, resented this sudden interference with his siesta time. I had been told previously of this practice of wart hogs in taking over old burrows and I knew that it was their habit to back down the hole, so that they could make a quick exit when necessary. This animal charged out of his hole with considerable force nearly overturning the vehicle and then set about the serious business of ripping up the tyre, which he obviously reckoned, had attacked him!

The survey gang and I sat helplessly in the vehicle watching, while pieces of tyre flew around us accompanied by grunts of satisfaction from the busy wart hog. Eventually, apparently satisfied with his efforts, he trotted off into the bush with his tail held high in the rather comical manner of his breed, leaving us to change the vehicle wheel, which, at this stage, was bereft of tyre and tube.

The second incident involved that most unlikely of African plain animals, the wildebeest. I suppose most of us have seen films of these strange and rather comical looking beasts galloping around the African plains, carrying out all sorts of strange antics and living up to their reputation as the animal comedian of this part of the world. In appearance they appear like a cross between an American bison and an antelope and they are generally considered to be a pretty harmless sort of animal, much prized as a good meal by prides of lions.

On this occasion, I was out of my vehicle, had set up my theodolite to take some sights and was directing the survey assistants where to set their tache staffs when a bull wildebeest suddenly appeared. He walked around me with much snorting and started to paw the ground in a manner reminiscent of a domestic bull. His circling began to close and I became suddenly aware that he was liable to charge at any moment. A quick look around for help convinced me that I was out of luck, as my survey team were heading for nearby trees. Deciding that discretion was the better part of valour in these circumstances, I left my theodolite and backed cautiously towards the nearest tree.

The wildebeest had apparently little interest in me as he immediately charged the theodolite, hooked it up and sent it flying into the air to land with an ominous crash of breaking glass some distance away. He then tossed back his head and with the air of someone a job well done, departed into the distance. Needless to say, the theodolite, an expensive instrument, had suffered considerable damage in the incident. I suppose I was a bit naive to think that the loss and damage forms that I subsequently had to submit in quintuplicate to my Head Office after this mishap would pass without comment! I suppose if the animal in question had been the notoriously short sighted and bad tempered black rhino, I would have had more hope of having my story readily accepted by a naturally sceptical Audit Department, who doubtless had heard many strange loss and damage stories in their time! Suffice it to say that it was many weeks before this matter was cleared up and the story made the rounds of the Public Works Department, leading to innumerable funny jokes at my expense!

Since we were working in the territory of the well-known nomad Masai tribe, it was inevitable that we would have contact with them and, in fact, it became an almost daily occurrence. The Masai tribe have been well documented over the years and they were, at this stage, still a truly nomad tribe moving across the flat bush country with their families and their beloved cattle as was necessary to get grazing and water for their stock. Their houses were made from frames of branches with animal skin or grass coverings and when they moved to another area, their house frames and other possessions were carried on the backs of donkeys.

They are a proud people of Nilotic origin with long thin faces and straight noses and are lighter in colour than many of the other tribes of Kenya. Perhaps the most disconcerting thing about them, from the white man's point of view, was their total contempt for our way of life. The young warriors armed with spears and short swords that travelled around in their Morani or age groups spoke little or no Swahili (the lingua franca of East Africa), had little time for the white man and considered that they were in every way superior to the other tribes of the country.

Our survey staff were frankly terrified of them and kept their distance from them whenever possible. As our survey proceeded it became necessary to move further and further away from civilisation and into the Masai country. It became commonplace for a pair of Masai Morani to appear in our camp in the early hours of the morning, as we loaded up our transport ready for a day's fieldwork. They would stand, leaning on their spears, often on one leg with the other foot wrapped round the spear haft, and watch us in complete silence while we made our preparations to leave. Then, at the last moment they would climb up into the back of the vehicle, spears and all, terrifying the life out of our survey assistants who huddled together out of their way. Our uninvited passengers spoke no Swahili, but neither did they do us any harm. During the day they stood watching our work and in the evening they climbed back on the vehicle, returned to camp with us and disappeared as mysteriously as the had come.

Clearly they were fascinated by what we were doing, particularly by our instrument work, as they often stood behind us as we took readings through our theodolites and sneaked up and looked through the telescope whenever they had a chance. I never found out exactly what was the purpose of their visits, but I presume their chief sent two of them every day to report back to him on what we were doing on their tribal lands. The District Commissioner would have briefed their chief on our project, but I expect the chief was still wary of what was going on in his territory.

Later, as the survey work neared the border of what was then Tanganyika, we were able to move camp to the comparative luxury of a small hotel situated at a village near the border called Namanga. Needless to say our Masai "escorts" turned up again in a few days and remained with us for the remainder of the project. Their "bush telegraph" was obviously very effective, as we had moved a good many miles from our previous camp.

We continued to work in this area for some weeks without many incidents, enjoying the hospitality of the hotel owners after our long sojourn in the bush. They owned a very large and handsome Rhodesian Ridgeback dog called Bruce to whom I became very attached and in my free time at weekends, he and I used to go for long walks in the bush.

On one such occasion we went climbing up one of those strange little volcanic intrusions, which one finds every now and again protruding out of the flat bushland country in Kenya. This hill was perhaps 500 foot high and covered in dense thorn scrub, but had well defined game tracks leading towards the summit. As Bruce and I made our way up the track, we came to a place where the path detoured round a large rock outcrop. Bruce stopped suddenly looking upwards and the hair on his back stood up and he growled ominously. Following his gaze I saw a troop of baboons was on the rock outcrop above us. The large male baboon began to bark and his troop joined in a chorus of roaring barks, which resonated around the hillside.

I had been regaled by our hosts with many stories of baboon behaviour, in particular their technique of encouraging a dog to attack them and then as the dog went for their throat, they would fall back and rip out its stomach with the claws of their powerful back legs. With these stories in mind I hung on to Bruce, who was a very powerful animal, with all my strength, while the baboons roared and he barked back at them and made every effort to attack them. Not wishing to give up my attempt to reach the summit, I picked up stones with my free hand and threw them at the baboons to try and scare them away. This it transpired was a serious mistake!

The old male, followed shortly by his troop, picked up sticks and stones and other unsavoury items and showered them down on us with renewed roars of rage. Needless to say, I was forced to beat an ignominious retreat down the hill, having learnt a serious lesson about the intelligence of the monkey population.

It was on this particular walk that I acquired a tick bite, which was to prove to be a carrier of the tick fever disease. In a matter of a few days, my leg became very swollen and painful and I started to run a high temperature. The nearest hospital was over a hundred miles away in Nairobi and it so happened that Anderson and the hotel manager and his wife had taken off for a few days holiday, and our driver was down with malaria so I had little alternative but to get in the old Bedford and drive myself to Nairobi. I do not recall much about that trip and I suppose it was hardly surprising since, when I arrived, it transpired that I had a temperature of 105 degrees. After two or three days of treatment things improved considerably and I was able to take notice of what was happening around me again and to realise that I was in good hands, particularly as many of the nursing sisters were Irish!

I believe it was on the night of my fourth day in

hospital that loud singing in a strong Scottish accent rudely awakened me and I found that I was about to get a new bed neighbour. Jock, as I was later to find out, had come in after two weeks in the bush and decided to have a good few nights celebrating his return to civilisation. He had made his way to a newly opened nightclub in Nairobi and there consumed large quantities of alcohol at the bar, which was on the third floor of the building. After some time he was, not unnaturally, overcome by a desire to relieve himself and set about searching for the nearest toilet. For some reason, known only to himself and relating to his inebriated state, he decided that the door leading into the lift shaft was the one he required. Unfortunately the lift had not yet been installed and this door was closed off with a timber barricade. Nothing daunted, Jock managed to remove the obstacle, opened the door and fell three floors down to the bottom of the empty lift shaft.

That he had survived to tell the tale was a quite remarkable feat and was presumably due to the fact that he was so drunk, that he fell in a totally relaxed condition and was thus able to hit the ground without fatal injury. Such was his state of intoxication however, that, although he had broken both arms and legs, several ribs and various less important bones, he apparently felt little or no pain for several hours - this in spite of the fact that the medical staff were unable to give him pain killers due to the amount of alcohol in his blood. The following day was a very different story for poor Jock! However, I believe he fully recovered from his injuries and was up and around again in a few weeks.

After my two-week sojourn in hospital I returned once again to Namanga to assist Anderson in the completion of his reconnaissance survey, which we managed to complete without any further major problems.

CHAPTER 3.
LIVING ON THE WILD SIDE

The first stage of the survey having being successfully completed, I returned to Head Office in Nairobi to work with Anderson on the finalisation of the new road alignment based on our survey in the field. When our bosses had finally approved this, I returned once again to the field with a Polish Surveyor called Stefan to set out and peg the final alignment.

This was my first experience of detail surveying a road in virgin country and I must confess that after the first week or two it became a rather tiresome chore. Due to the fact that, there was at this time no detailed ordinance survey of the country, there were no Survey Beacons or levelling benchmarks to tie into a survey. This meant that, when we went out with our instruments setting out traverse surveys, it was necessary to close back the survey to the starting point every day, in order to ensure that we had made no errors. If, it transpired there was an error, then the whole section of survey had to be repeated until we got it correct.

We started our work just after dawn, since the heat haze by 10 a.m. became such that it was nearly impossible to read through an instrument after this time. The magnification of the telescopes made the staff readings jump around too much to make accurate readings possible. The remainder of the working day was then spent in plotting the day's work on paper.

Those who have never camped out in Africa might find it hard to imagine how relatively luxurious bush camps could be made. We slept in what were designated "Government Senior Officers Tents". I was not by any means a Senior Government Officer, but I suppose since we had to spend so much time out in the bush the Ministry had obtained permission for junior engineers in the Roads Branch to occupy this type of accommodation. These tents were of a size, which could easily take two camp beds and our tin trunks. They had canvas floors and were fitted with an outer canvas roof which came forward of the door to make a front veranda. Here we had our table and chairs for meals and work. Since there was a clear air space between the tent roof and the outer canvas, the tents were comparatively cool for sleeping in at night, an essential requirement in low land areas such as this, where the nights could remain very hot and muggy. At the back of the tents was fitted a semi-circular canvas extension, which also had a canvas floor and here we had a canvas bath and washbasin which could be folded away when not in use. The bath was, naturally, not very large in size and it was square in shape, but it provided a very necessary function, when one returned covered in dust from work in the field. Toilets were made at each new campsite by digging holes and surrounding them with a canvas sheet.

One of the things we had to watch out for in camp tents was the possibility of finding a snake comfortably asleep in your clothes, or a scorpion resting in your shoes. It became routine to shake out your shoes before putting them on in the morning and to lift up your clothes with circumspection before dressing. In fact scorpions in your shoes were quite a common occurrence. It is hard to imagine why they hid here unless they enjoyed the smell of sweaty feet! Snakes were fortunately not so common in this part of the country and I can recall only two occasions in my twenty-six years in Africa when I had narrow escapes from snakebite.

On the first such occasion I picked up a puff adder with my shirt one morning, but fortunately dropped it in time. The second occasion occurred when I was hunting a buck in heavy bush for meat for the staff. I was passing under a thorn tree, when a small green mamba fell off the tree and ended up down the back of my shirt. Because of the heat, I was wearing my shirt outside my shorts and the snake, which appeared to be as scared of me as I was of it, wriggled down my back and took off without biting me.

Water was sometimes a problem in camp and where it was not available near the campsite; it had to be carted in drums. Food was bought in the nearest small shop or "duka", often situated some miles away and usually run by an Asian family. We subsisted largely on tinned items augmented occasionally with venison, guinea fowl or francolin (a type of bush partridge), if we were in an area where we were allowed to shoot for the pot. Our staff lived on their traditional diet of maize meal mixed with any vegetables they could get and meat from anything we were able to shoot for them. The two of us shared a camp servant who made the beds, did the washing and cooked for us. African men servants were incredibly adaptable and had the ability to produce an excellent meal in a very short time, cooked over an open fire with the help of a Primus stove.

Nightfall came soon after 6 p.m., with little variation during the year, in a country so near the Equator, so we ate, drank and read by the lights of pressure paraffin lamps and having been up since dawn, it was usually not later than 9 p.m. by the time we retired to our camp beds. I lived for the best part of two years of my life as a junior engineer in field camps and they were happy years in spite of the relatively primitive conditions in which we existed.

From an engineering point of view it was incredibly good experience in the field of road survey. This experience subsequently stood me in good stead when I became senior and mostly desk bound. I have seen so many senior engineers in difficulties with directing field work, particularly those young African graduates who, on their return from graduation overseas, were being placed in senior positions without first gaining the desirable field experience.

When I finally became a Branch Head in the Ministry of Works, I made myself fairly unpopular at times by sending out young African graduate engineers to work in the field soon after they arrived. Many of them felt that this was rather below the dignity of their newly acquired qualifications, but I hope that in the end they appreciated that I did it in their best interests.

Not unnaturally living in these field conditions with a staff that had little or no English one had to learn Swahili quite quickly. I soon became able to communicate verbally with to our African staff and was able to share their feelings and to admire, in particular, their cheerful approach to an existence, which placed them far away from their families and even their own tribal areas for many months of the year.

Our staff came from several different tribes, mainly big Jaluo from the hot plains surrounding Lake Victoria, Wakamba from south of Nairobi and Kikuyu from the fertile lands north of Nairobi. They were on the whole a cheerful and willing lot who were united in their fear that a Masai warrior might stick a spear in them one day, if they unwittingly gave them cause! This was not an entirely unjustifiable fear, in view of the contempt in which the Masai held everyone who was not of their tribe.

The Masai were, as most people these days are aware, celebrated in days gone by for their lion hunts. Apparently, on these occasions they surrounded a male lion and goaded it into charging one of their circle by slowly closing in and shouting insults at it. The warrior at whom the lion charged crouched down behind his large shield and tried to impale the lion with his long slender spear. If he was successful, then the rest of the Moran jumped in and finished off the beast. If he was unsuccessful, then he was either killed or badly mauled before the lion escaped.

It was a fact of life that when these nomad tribes moved with their cattle to another grazing area, any sick or badly injured who could not walk or keep up with the rest of the clan, were often left behind to die or be killed by hyenas or other animals. This was their tradition and apparently accepted stoically by the unfortunates involved

On finalisation of this survey and fieldwork I returned once again to the "flesh pots" of Nairobi and the company of my friends in Thika Roadhouse.

My next project was supervising the construction of two large box culverts on the Kiambu road. This road was being upgraded and since the project was near to Nairobi, I was able to travel to site on a daily basis from the Roadhouse. Kiambu was a very different part of Kenya from the thorn bush of Masailand. European settlers who, at this time, were enjoying a boom in the price of coffee farmed the area. As a result they were living in a life style, which, to me, was unbelievably luxurious. Many of them had two or three very expensive motorcars and some of them had their own private aeroplanes in which they frequently flew down to the Coast to live it up in the hotels and on the beaches around Mombasa. I found them exceedingly hospitable people and many of them certainly threw their money around with little thought for the future, or so, at least, it seemed to us poor civil servants!

Of course, it is a well-known fact that many of

these older settlers had lived through hard times in the early days of settlement. At that time they had to struggle to make a living in climatic conditions that produced every kind of pest imaginable to attack their crops, not to mention the wild animals that were ready to feed on their harvests when they did succeed in producing them.

My boss at this time was an Irish engineer who had spent many years abroad and was one of the most likeable and helpful persons that it has ever been my privilege to work under. Always courteous, understanding and ready to assist young engineers with their problems, he was also extremely popular socially. This ability to mix with everyone meant he was able to provide a very useful link between the expatriate settler community, with their rather flamboyant lifestyle and the young expatriate colonial civil servants who, in comparison, lived in an austere world where spending money was often in short supply. In fact, I can recall that we used to confine ourselves to drinking Coca-Cola during the week, in order to save sufficient money to be able to take out a girl on the weekend! In retrospect, I suppose this probably saved us from acquiring ulcers in later years and so had benefits, which we did not appreciate at the time!

At this stage of Kenya's development most of the hospitals were staffed with young European nursing sisters, so it was only natural that these girls became our main social contacts. Almost inevitably most of these girls were of Scottish or Irish descent and they were a great bunch that had adapted in the most amazing fashion to working, in many cases, in very primitive conditions in small local hospitals. The Irish and Scots have always had a tradition of working in far-away places, partly because their own countries produced far more trained staff than they could absorb at home, but also, I believe, because we have a genuine urge to travel and work outside our own countries. Probably many of us would do so even if it were not an economic necessity.

I have always been amazed at the relatively few Englishmen one meets in the professions in developing countries. One might have been forgiven for thinking that the British Empire (as it existed in those days) was largely run at professional level by the Scots and the Irish! This was not true, of course, of the Colonial Administration. Provincial Commissioners, District Commissioners, District Officers etc. were, practically without exception, recruited from the ranks of Oxford and Cambridge graduates. Strangely enough, the Welsh as a nation do not appear to work abroad nearly as much as the other inhabitants of the British Isles and I can recall meeting very few Welshmen during my twenty-five years in Africa.

There was a feeling amongst the professionals in the Colonial Service that the Administration considered itself rather superior to us and they tended to keep to themselves. When you consider that, in a Provincial Headquarters, we all belonged to the same club and in such a small community tended to see each other nearly every day, the situation was really rather farcical and quite unnecessary. I am afraid that, as is so often the case, the wives of these officers tended to be the ringleaders in this social segregation.

After independence, however, the situation became very different, as it was the administrative officers who found themselves in difficulties in obtaining alternative employment. Consultants who moved in to replace the expatriate professional permanent staff in these countries during that period (a time when local professional staff were undergoing third level education) were not slow to offer employment to those officers who had experience of the country.

CHAPTER 4. .
BACK TO CIVILISATION

To return to my own life, after the new road structures were successfully completed on the Kiambu road, I took two weeks of local leave and in the company of three Irish friends and one English friend, took off for a holiday at the Coast.

The road to Mombasa at this time had not been tarmac surfaced and the surface consisted of a variety of different gravels and sandy materials in varying stages of roughness. As was the traditional way, we travelled by night to escape the heat of the day. It was a long and tiring journey. On this particular occasion we were lucky enough to arrive safely without major incident, a fairly considerable feat considering the age of the vehicle, which belonged to one of the party. The brakes of the old car had, in fact, almost ceased to function by the time we had descended to the Coast.

I was to discover in later times, during many trips taken on duty on this road, that there were many unexpected hazards to be met along the way.

The road was crossed at regular intervals by small watercourses, which during the dry season produced only a trickle of water, but during the rains became raging torrents, which would have required major bridging to keep them passable. Since money was not available for this purpose, these watercourses were provided with concrete causeways that were called

"Irish bridges" or "drifts." These could be easily crossed by vehicles in the dry season, but provided major hazards in the rainy season.

Then one had the option of taking a chance and driving through the stream or waiting on one side in the hopes that the flood would drop to a reasonable level in a short time to allow safe crossing. This waiting period could be several hours, or even require an overnight stay in your vehicle on occasion. Any effort to turn back would usually be frustrated by the presence of another drift, which had been passable previously, but was now under water. Situated as they were in areas abounding in all kinds of big game, the enforced stay at these drifts could provide some interesting and scary moments.

On one such occasion, whilst on a bridge survey, I met an Italian family who had spent several unhappy hours in their vehicle at an impassable drift surrounded by a pack of African wild dogs. The dogs apparently stayed with them in a silent circle and as time went on the circle grew smaller as the dogs closed in closer and closer until, finally, after several frightening hours, they gave up and went on their way. I imagine that the family were in no great danger so long as they stayed in their vehicle, but when I arrived on the scene shortly after the departure of the animals, I quickly became surrounded by a shouting, weeping, and hysterical Italian family. Clearly they believed that they had been lucky to escape with their lives from being savaged to death by a pack of wild dogs! In fact, I believe that African Wild Dogs do not usually attack humans, but possibly this pack was near starvation and could have been serious in their intentions.

I heard of another occasion when a family in a car, stuck at a drift in similar circumstances, were visited by a playful pride of lions that gambolled round their car. At one stage one of the lionesses actually jumped onto the roof of the car and sat there for a short time, while the petrified passengers cowered inside expecting the roof of the car to collapse at any moment.

Elephants were commonly met walking along the road and indeed often blocked the road temporarily by leaving the branches of trees lying in the carriageway. They had little respect for drivers and it was quite common to have to stop and wait while a herd of elephants meandered along the road in front of you, pulling down young branches of trees to feed on as they went. Tooting the horn at these animals was not to be recommended, as the usual result was that the herd leader would turn round, lift his trunk, bring his huge ears forward and show every sign of getting ready to make a charge. The unfortunate motorist then found himself in the situation of deciding whether to back up or sit tight and hope for the best.

As I found out, in later times, after meeting and talking with game rangers, most charges made by elephants on these occasions were "mock charges", intended to scare off the intruders and seldom pressed home. However, it would obviously be foolish for inexperienced persons to make such an assumption in case they turned out to be wrong on that particular occasion!

My personal worst moment with elephants on the Mombasa road happened on a day when I was driving home and found myself suddenly following behind a small elephant calf that had appeared out of the bush in front of me. Seeing me, the calf galloped off down the road in front of the car and as I slowly followed behind I heard the trumpeting scream of an enraged elephant behind me. Looking back, I saw, to my horror, mother elephant bearing down on me. Caught, as I was, in a sandwich between them, I had little option but to carry on slowly down the road while the calf ran in front of me and mother came up rapidly behind! Very fortunately, a bend appeared in the road ahead and the calf went straight on into the bush, whilst I was able to shoot round the corner and thankfully see, through my rear mirror, mother elephant disappearing after her young!

To return to the story of my first road trip to Mombasa; we duly arrived in the city in the early hours of the morning and took up our rooms in the Nyali Beach Hotel and flaked out for some hours before heading for the beach and our first taste of the Indian Ocean. We had a wonderful holiday, the sun shone, we goggle-fished, we swam, we drank too much, we chased the girls and some of us got badly sunburned! One of our party was red-haired and had the very white skin, which is often found with this hair colour and he suffered very badly with sunburn for several days after this holiday. In this part of the world the reflective heat off the sea is sufficiently strong to burn your skin even through a cotton shirt, so it is necessary to great care if you do not want to spend the rest of your holiday badly sunburnt.

Our eventual return to Nairobi was fairly uneventful, but it was quite a nasty shock to have to return to work in the P.W.D. offices after such an idyllic holiday and I think it took all of us a few days to settle back into the old routine.

It was not long before I was off on safari again, this time to work with two experienced road surveyors, one of whom was Polish and one Italian. Our project was to finalise a new road alignment in the Kenya Highlands from a place called Molo to Mau Summit, which as its name implies was high in the hills of the European farming area. It was intended by our superiors that we would be accommodated in Government standard tents for this project, but thanks to the kindness of the local veterinary surgeon and his wife, we ended up living in a thatched "rondavel" on their farm.

Rondavels were circular buildings based on a design used by many African tribes. The true African type of this building is constructed of a timber pole frame roofed with grass and plastered with a mixture of mud and cow dung, whilst the floor is constructed from much the same material. The roof rises to a conical point and cooking and heating are carried out in an open fire in the middle of the hut, the smoke escaping through the roof apex. Light and ventilation are provided by square openings in the sidewalls with wooden shutters to keep out the cold at night, a very necessary precaution in the Highlands of Kenya where night frosts are common. Not unnaturally the true African hut is a dark and smoky place where the occupants squat round the fire and thus escape the rising smoke and sleep on couch beds made from branches around the perimeter walls.

A more sophisticated version of this accommodation with walls made of shaped concrete block and a concrete floor is commonly used in many parts of Africa for guestrooms in hotels and on farms. These buildings can provide very sensible accommodation, remaining cool during the heat of the day and warm at night, extra heating, where necessary, being provided by an open fireplace in one corner.

The guest rondavel we were lucky enough to be able to occupy was of this superior type and I still remember how good the couple that owned it were to us during this time. We lived comfortably in this rondavel for the duration of the project and since we were in the "White Highlands" as they were known at that time, fresh vegetables and meat was readily obtainable and gave us a pleasant change from the basic tinned food or venison, which was the normal staple diet on safari.

The area was heavily wooded and since our rondavel was sited near a forested area, the cold nights were filled with strange animal noises. The most hair-raising of these was the call of the tree hyrax, a strange animal like a cross between a hare and a small bear, which lived in the trees, presumably on a diet of leaves. The hyrax call starts like somebody winding up an alarm clock and then ends with a most eerie banshee scream. It certainly took a lot of getting used to, particularly as one of them apparently spent most of its nights sitting on the roof of our rondavel calling to its friends!

The Kikuyu tribe considered the tree hyrax a great delicacy for eating purposes and trapped them in snares. Our houseboy told me that if a hyrax bites you, the only way to release his hold is by cutting off his head. This, he maintained, was because his teeth grow facing inwards and consequently he cannot release his jaws after biting. How true this was I did not know and certainly did not intend to find out!

I must admit that I did feel like murdering our roof resident on several occasions! We saw hyrax on one or two occasions running across the ground to get from one tree to another and they were most ungainly to look at on the ground, proceeding with a strange gait due to the back legs being far longer than the front. Our Kikuyu servants also told us that hyrax had a pocket in the middle of their backs where they kept their young, but I never saw one dead, so I do not know if this was true. The cousin of the tree hyrax, the rock hyrax was a different animal altogether. About the size of a rabbit, they lived on the ground in hot dry places and could often be seen lying out in the sun on rocky hillsides.

Leopards were frequently around our camp at

night and our farmer friends kept their dogs locked away safely at night, as dogs were considered to be one of the leopard's favourite foods. On one occasion we spent a rather sleepless night as a leopard arrived outside our hut and spent some considerable time banging against the rondavel door, presumably because he smelt food inside. He then found some bones lying around the camp and proceeded to crunch these up noisily before departing elsewhere.

CHAPTER 5.
UP IN THE HIGHLANDS

Our survey work on this project was very different to what I had experienced on the hot Masai plains south of Nairobi.

This new road alignment ran through thick forest country and survey involved endless cutting of trace lines through this on either side of the proposed road centre line (which had been laid out previously in the reconnaissance survey) in order to take theodolite shots. These, when calculated out, would allow us to plot the contours of the land.

The work was slow and hard on the survey crew, but since we were at an altitude of over 8000 feet, at least the climate was cooler except in the middle of the day. At night, it became very cold and frost was quite common.

We were working in an area that was in the heartland of white settlement farming and here the farmers, as well as ranching cattle, grew wheat and coffee. At this time, all these crops appeared to be in high demand and the farming community was experiencing a boom, which left the settlers with money to burn, and they certainly took advantage of this situation and lived the good life to the full.

In fairness it must be said that most of them had had a very rough time in the early days when they had to contend with crop diseases, wild animals and untrained labour. Anyway, at this stage in the country's development, they were able to afford to keep expensive cars. These were mostly American imports, as these seemed better designed to survive the battering they received on the corrugated gravel and earth surfaced roads, which comprised the main transport routes of the country at this time. Their main social events centred on their clubs where they disported themselves during the weekends and much heavy drinking took place.

Some of the settlers also had their own aeroplanes and at least one of the clubs, to which I was once invited, had its own airstrip and here some of the Members indulged in what seemed to me to be dangerous aerial games of follow-my-leader. This was accomplished by using their 'planes to take off, fly around, land, and take off again one behind the other. We, relatively poor civil servants, were unable to compete with their living standards, but I must say that they were very good to us and we were quite often asked out to meals to the farms during weekends.

One day when we were working away in the forest area, I came on a cleft stick set in a cut line with a terse message stuck in the cleft. The message said, "This is the highest point. From here the road falls downward in both directions."

Obviously, an initial survey had come this way in the past. I found the message quite amusing at the time, as it was placed on the top of a hill with a view below the forest of perhaps two miles in either direction to the farmlands below! It was certainly a case of pointing out the obvious in a big way!

I realised after a short time, that I was fated to be cast in the role of peacemaker between an emotional Italian and an equally emotional Pole! The Pole like many of his unfortunate countrymen had escaped from

Poland, joined the British Army after the German invasion of his country, and had to leave his family behind. At the end of the war Russia had taken over his country and in these circumstances, he was afraid to return home, as he felt he would not be allowed to leave it again. In consequence, he was cut off from his family and it seemed likely that he might never be reunited with them again.

He liked to bait the Italian by commenting that the Italian troops would never stand and fight, but always ran away on these occasions. The Italian nearly always rose to the bait and riposted that the Pole was no one to talk, since he was not man enough to go back to Poland and find his family.

This unpleasant situation arose usually when both of them had, what is known in Ireland as "having drink taken" and it often ended in the Pole bursting into tears and retiring to his bed! I would then be left with the two of them not speaking to each other the following day until I was able to persuade them to shake hands and become friends again. Fortunately this situation eventually resolved itself when the Italian was sent off to carry out an urgent survey job elsewhere.

Eventually this survey was satisfactorily completed and I found myself back in the P.W.D. Head Office in Nairobi. Here, I was given the job of plotting up the field work for final alignment on this and other projects until, my contract having been completed, I departed on vacation leave, scheduled to return after leave as a member of the permanent staff. It was about this time that what had for many years been the Public Works Department was being re-named as the Ministry of Works. This represented a change in name only, as far as most of the ordinary professional staff were concerned, as only the Administration were affected by having a Minister appointed full time to head this new Ministry.

CHAPTER 6.
BACK TO THE FLESHPOTS OF NAIROBI

There is not much to be said about my first leave. Those friends whom I had made from the early days in Thika Road House had also completed their first tour and we all went home on the same ship, which made for a very pleasant journey. Having been on contract we all had our gratuities in our pockets, so, for a short time at least; we felt rich and spent plenty of money!

On return to my home in County Dublin, I did all the right things about seeing the relations and then I took off to U.K. and visited the home of one of my good friends who lived near Birmingham. I went down to London with him and had a few good days entertainment before returning to Ireland and getting in some trout fishing.

Our leave lasted for some three months, a long time to be doing nothing! I think most of us were quite pleased to get back to Kenya at this stage and settle back to life in the Thika Roadhouse and our Nairobi workplace. On my return, I found myself moved to the Materials Branch of the Ministry. The work of this Branch involved the testing of soils and all civil engineering materials, such as bitumen, concrete and reinforcing steel, which were used in construction work.

There was also a fair amount of outside fieldwork to be done in testing soils and gravels for settlement and compaction in the proposed foundations for buildings, roads and bridges. I thoroughly enjoyed this work, particularly that relating to soil mechanics, which was a very new science at that time.

An added interest was that this Branch also provided a consultancy service outside the Ministry, so one was able to meet and work with other engineers working in the private field.

I met with some interesting experiences on my field trips. On one occasion, for some reason, which I cannot now recall, I was sent with a team of operators to drill boreholes in the surface of Lake Magadi. This was a lake which was covered for a great part of its surface with a thick crust of soda, so thick, in fact, that it was possible in most parts at the dry season to drive a vehicle on it without going through the crust. We duly set up the rig on the crust and started drilling to remove samples. We had not, however, anticipated what was going to happen because of our drilling activities!

We set out to drill four holes some one hundred feet apart and as we started to recover the core samples from the fourth hole, water started to seep up through the boreholes and spread rapidly over the surface dissolving the soda crust. As you may imagine we removed the rig and ourselves from the lake surface a good deal faster than we had come in and I had to inform the Chief Materials Engineer that this project was not very feasible. We did, however, return at a later date and manage to get the necessary samples by spacing our boreholes a good deal further apart and leaving the site before the flow of water became a problem.

Later, I was sent down the Nairobi to Mombasa road to a place called Makindu where a new road alignment had been surveyed and pegged and a bridge site identified for a river crossing. Bridges had to be constructed and completed well before the road construction so that the earthworks of the road embankments up to the bridge could be safely placed and compacted.

My job was to investigate the soil where the bridge foundations would be placed to see what type of material lay below the surface. If the material was poor, then it might be necessary to drive piles down to more solid material or, in some extreme circumstances, to move the whole road alignment to a better crossing site. This particular site was in a rather swampy location and when I arrived at the site with the drilling crew, I found there was a nice shady tree just where the alignment was planned to cross. Standing under the shade of this tree, was a large black cow rhino with her calf beside her.

I was aware at this stage of my time in Kenya that the black rhino was more short- tempered and in consequence, more aggressive than the white rhino, so I approached the site with some caution. Eventually I succeeded with the help of the African crew by shouting and throwing stones at her to get her to move away, which she finally did at a brisk trot with her small tail stuck up in the air and her calf trotting beside her.

Returning to work next day, we found rhino and calf had ensconced themselves once again under the tree and the operation had to be repeated. This happened every day for the next week. I did, however, find out on the third day, purely by a lucky accident, that the rhino would charge at virtually any object, such as a piece of paper, if it flew past her short-sighted vision. I therefore adopted the successful tactic of daily shinning up a nearby tree upwind and throwing pieces of paper into the air, which would fly past her nose and galvanise her into charging after it. We would then quickly take possession of the site.

Fortunately, after the second week the sight of the equipment and no doubt, the human scent became too much for Mrs Rhino and she moved elsewhere, leaving us in possession of the site for the remainder of the project. I stayed during the period of this investigation in a small roadside hotel owned and managed by a retired white hunter whose name, by curious coincidence was Hunter, in fact the establishment was called Hunter's Hotel. When he realised my great interest in the local wildlife, I had many fascinating talks with Mr Hunter about his experiences in Kenya and he told me many interesting tales.

One that I particularly remember, was about how young Masai warriors used to play a dangerous game with rhinos in order to show off their courage. A group of warriors would find a rhino and annoy him into charging one of them (not a difficult feat with a black rhino!). At the last moment, the warrior in question would leap aside or even jump over the rhino and whack it on the nose just behind the horn. If he managed to hit the right spot the rhino would apparently fall down unconscious, and the warrior would receive great acclaim. If he missed, then he and his companions would have to climb quickly up the nearest tree and wait until the enraged animal got tired and left!

Mr. Hunter took me out in his safari truck on a few occasions in the late evening or the early morning and showed me many species of the big game in which the area abounded. He knew every rhino in the area and had given all names. We drove up to them in the bush in his battered safari wagon and I was able to see them at close range. In fact, sometimes we seemed too close for comfort!

His vehicle had old lorry tyres tied to the sides like the fenders on a ship. It was only when I went out with him for the first time, that I realised the reason for these fenders was to absorb the charge of his "pet" rhinos when they got annoyed with his presence, which happened periodically.

On these occasions, his technique was to drive away as fast as possible and if the rhino caught up with him, he would at the last moment pull hard over so that the rhino hit only a glancing blow off the tyre fenders on the side of the vehicle. It happened once when I was with him and I can assure you I did not enjoy the experience of being chased and hit by a two-ton rhino. The Game Rangers in the back of the vehicle, however, appeared to thoroughly enjoy the entertainment. My host remarked, casually, as we drove away that Gertrude appeared to be in a bad temper that day.

On another expedition, my host took me out on a trip to see buffalo in the Reserve. Having travelled some miles through the bush in early morning darkness, we finally stopped and awaited the dawn, always a wonderful time of the day in Africa, as the bush slowly comes to life as the sun rises in a clear sky.

On this occasion, however, as the sky lightened, I suddenly realised that we were parked within a few feet of an enormous herd of African Buffalo, all of whom were standing shoulder to shoulder facing the vehicle in a way, that, to me at least, appeared very menacing indeed! I suppose, in fact, that they were well used to seeing the Warden's vehicle at such close quarters, because they gradually went back to feeding and wandered away, finally disappearing into the cool of the nearby forest, where they would spend the hot hours of the day.

I felt quite sad when the time came to leave Hunter's Hotel and return to Nairobi, but it had been a most interesting time and I could look forward to the work of testing the materials I had accumulated and writing my report on the bridge site project. This was something, which I always found a stimulating engineering exercise.

CHAPTER 7.
CAME THE SOUTH AFRICANS

At this stage of Kenya's development, the Ministry of Works had received large loan funds from, I believe, the World Bank and was, at last, in a position to make a really good start in developing the road network of the Country.

Since enough trained local technical and professional staff were unavailable, a large contingent, (at least fifty, I believe I was told at the time) of South African Road Engineers, Supervisors and other roads staff down to the level of Road Foremen and Plant Operators were recruited by the Government.

Suddenly there was a new South African Chief Roads Engineer and before long a South African Deputy Chief Roads Engineer replaced the retiring British engineers occupying these positions and the Branch staff rapidly expanded with South Africans occupying most of the new posts. I was, at the time, a very junior road engineer, so I do not really know why these posts were nearly all filled by South Africans.

I would presume, that, it was felt that South Africans had road building experience in similar types of conditions and British engineers with the right experience may have been difficult to recruit at this time, which was shortly after the end of World War II.

And so, one day, I found myself once again on the road to Mombasa, accompanying a Senior Roads Engineer with a convoy of Land Rovers and other vehicles. Our job was to meet the specially chartered ship, which was carrying a large contingent of the new junior staff recruited in South Africa, and deliver them back to our bosses in Nairobi.

When we arrived in Mombasa, we found that the ship we were to meet had already docked and our new South African staff had been lodged in various hotels around the town. As we rounded them up, we found that many of the more junior personnel had Afrikaans as their first language and, in consequence, spoke and understood very little English. This, as could be expected, led to some problems in dealing with them in the early stages. From the level of Supervisor down, they were a very tough and hardy bunch and they were certainly not used to being in a country where the white man was not the complete boss! Their wives were in the same mould and one way and another most of them were intent on having as good a time as possible in Mombasa for the period of their stay.

The Police force of Mombasa had more or less given up trying to control their drinking spree and it was a good two days before we were able to round them all up and get the convoy on its way back up the Mombasa – Nairobi road.

In later days, it was my job to work in the field with these tough Afrikaners and I had nothing but admiration for their abilities, both as Supervisors and machine operators. They had an extraordinary ability to get the best of production from their African staff and most of the field staff accepted their rough justice in a way that I do not believe they would have accepted it, from those of us who came from Europe.

Kenya, at this time, had very few trained African plant operators, foremen or mechanics, certainly nothing like enough to fulfil the requirements of the new development programme. These posts were now filled by the new arrivals and they proved a great asset to the Ministry. They were prepared to live a nomad life, with their wives and families, in caravans or other temporary accommodation, in the most remote parts of Kenya and accept conditions that, I know, most other white staff would not accept.

As the development of the country's infrastructure proceeded, the Ministry set up a Road Field Training Unit, which, in the course of time, came under my charge and a picked bunch of these same South African Operators, Foremen and Supervisors became responsible for training African staff to do their jobs. Not an easy task for persons who must have known that they were doing themselves out of a job in the long run, but they carried it out extremely well. So well, in fact, that by the time that Kenya gained its Independence, all Roads Staff posts up to the level of Supervisor were filled by Africans, and several local Road Engineers were under training.

The Afrikaners were, in the main, very large and heavily built men, who probably reflected their Dutch ancestry, and their Supervisors ruled their own staff with a rod of iron. On more than one occasion, I have seen an Afrikaans Foreman or Plant Operator from a Field Construction Unit appear with a fine black eye and bruised face on a Monday morning. Discipline was enforced the hard way with their own people, and one learned not to ask questions as to why and wherefore!

We found that the favourite drink of the South African staff was their brandy and fairly potent stuff it was, as I found out to my cost on more than one occasion! Every once in a while, all the Afrikaans staff with their wives and families would have a get together, when they would have a barbecue and consume large quantities of brandy. Following this, we would have some absenteeism for a day or two, after which some rather sorry looking gentlemen would reappear and things would return to normal. Many of the Afrikaners were excellent rifle shots and I suppose, had been brought up on farms where antelope of various species were plentiful. In these circumstances, a proportion of the game would have had to be shot, in order to keep them down to a level where they did not interfere with the grazing for the cattle and growing of crops which was their livelihood. This would have given them plenty of opportunity to develop their shooting skills and gave us some headaches when they were posted in areas of Kenya where game of all kinds was plentiful.

I remember one particular instance where a Game Warden reported to me that one of my road foremen had shot a rhino in the Game Reserve. I called the foreman in and asked if it was true. It transpired that he had taken a small .22 rifle out early one morning to shoot a few guinea fowl for the pot. Unexpectedly he came on a rhino and apparently could not resist firing at it. It seems hard to believe that anyone with such a small calibre rifle could kill a two-ton rhino, but this is what had happened. The Warden told me that the rhino had been shot five times through the eye and in a small circle round the eye and this had allowed at least one bullet to reach the animals brain, killing it almost instantly. This standard of shooting would require quite remarkable marksmanship.

The marksman said to me in his English Afrikaans:

"Christ, man, I am so sorry, but I could not resist shooting at it when I came on it so suddenly!"

He was fined and severely reprimanded and learned his lesson, but this, I believe, was only one of several incidents that occurred in the early stages of the settling in period for the new staff.

I returned to Nairobi Head Office after our Mombasa recruitment exercise and settled back into the old routine of soils testing. The rains came and one day, as I stood in the entrance to the Soils Laboratory hoping that the pouring rain to ease up so that I could make a dash for my transport, I witnessed a most peculiar phenomenon.

I have, subsequently, seen this phenomenon again in Africa, but have never heard it properly explained. As I waited, there came a sudden and alarming crash of thunder, followed closely by a terrific fork of lightning that hit the lightning conductor on the corrugated iron roof. Then three "balls" of fire, totally round and perhaps three feet in diameter, bounced off the roof like enormous tennis balls and then bounced across the yard and slammed one after the other into some 40 gallon drums full of petrol which were stacked in a corner of the yard.

Strangely enough, that was the end of the story. Why the petrol drums did not explode I do not know, nor can I find an explanation for the "balls of fire", but clearly, they were the product of the lightning strike.

The second such phenomenon, I saw many years later whilst working in Lesotho. On this occasion, I awoke to another fierce thunderstorm looked out of the window and saw a fork of lightning strike an electric pole transformer, which was sited on the road just outside our garden. The transformer burst into flames and produced a fireworks display for some time afterwards. Immediately after the strike, however, two balls of fire bounced down from the pole transformer, bounced across our garden, and disappeared.

It is perhaps difficult for people living in the British Isles to imagine the ferocity of these thunderstorms, which are common in Africa. I doubt if any of us working in that continent, ever became used to them. They could be quite terrifying and extremely dangerous if you were in the wrong place at the time and inevitably, all electric power failed at such times, which did not help the situation. I remember a very nice young English technician in the telephone service, who had lost a leg in an accident, telling me how terrified he was when a thunderstorm suddenly broke out whilst he was working on a new link station on a hill. His fear related to the fact that his false leg was made of metal and he was sure that the next lightning strike would hit his false leg!

Being seated in a car during a thunderstorm is apparently quite a safe place to be as the car tyres insulate the vehicle from the ground. Many years after we had left Kenya and I was working in Lesotho, I was told of a motorist driving on the road from Lesotho to Johannesburg that had his vehicle struck by lightening and was left unharmed inside his car, but all the tyres and the clutch had been burned away!

CHAPTER 8.
I HIT THE HOT SPOTS

It was about this time that the move for independence in Kenya, which had long been desired, began to take on a violent aspect and significant numbers of the large and dominant Kikuyu tribe took oaths to kill all Europeans and their local supporters.

So started what became known as the Mau Mau rebellion, which eventually achieved its aim when Independence was declared at the end of 1963. It was a time when many unpleasant things happened, as I suppose is inevitable in this type of guerrilla warfare. It certainly did not assist in my career as an engineer and the Mau Mau Rebellion has been well documented by several writers elsewhere, so I do not intend to dwell any further on this period of my time in Kenya.

My next posting was as Executive Engineer, Ministry of Works, in the Coastal Province of Mombasa. The duties of an Executive Engineer were to be a personal assistant to the Provincial Engineer and take over a proportion of his administrative and professional duties and act for him when he was on local leave or away on duty. In the coastal M.O.W. Offices in Mombasa, my job was, in many ways, quite an idealistic existence, apart from the everlasting sticky heat, which was hard to bear in days before air conditioning became the norm.

At this time, the large passenger ships still provided the main transport system for personnel around the world, and one of the most popular duties of the Executive Engineer in the Ministry of Works, was to meet senior staff members on their return from, or departure on, vacation leave!

In either case, this involved going on board the passenger liners and either ensuring that they were happily accommodated or meeting them on their arrival, taking them off the ship and seeing them away on the train for Nairobi. Since the bars on these ships remained open, duty free, whilst the vessel was in port a good time was assured for all concerned!

In fact, parties at night on these liners were a cheap and regular form of entertainment that could be enjoyed by any expatriate whilst the ship remained in Mombasa Harbour. The evenings were always pleasant on shipboard, as there was a cool sea breeze compared to the interior of our Government houses, where fans provided little solace from the sweltering heat that persisted for most of the year.

The heat also made unexpected difficulties working in the office, as perspiration from one's hands and arms seemed to get everywhere and paper stuck to your hands when you tried to move it. You tended to sit as still as possible at your desk with your back well away from the chair back, otherwise you immediately stuck to the back of the chair.

As far as I can recall the office hours were from 7.30 a.m. to 12 noon and again from 2 p.m. to 4 p.m. Lunch would be after a shower and clothes change and some expatriates had a siesta after lunch, before returning to the office. Personally, I found it impossible to work satisfactorily after a siesta at lunchtime. The indigenous population was far more sensible in this respect, and just retired to their cool thatched houses from midday until the sun began to get lower in the sky.

Mombasa, being very close to the Equator, meant that the times of sunset and sunrise were virtually unchanged throughout the year and both occurred with a suddenness that was quite strange to us, who are used to long twilight before darkness.

The local tribes of African origin in the Coastal Area were cheerful, happy and easygoing people. They lived at this time on good terms with a mixed population, which included Arabs, Indians and Europeans with a sprinkling of half-castes of all these races. There existed also a small population of expatriate "drop outs" who lived in a sort of fashion along the beaches.

The tropical climate produced luxuriant growth of all kinds and meant that food crops grew fast and easily. Clearly it was possible for the local population to live a fairly easy life with plenty of available fish, an abundance of tropical fruit and vegetables and miles of sandy beaches fringed by coconut palms.

The main business of Mombasa centred on the Port and the import and export of goods by ship up and down the East Coast of Africa and the Arab dhows that sailed across and back to the Middle East using the monsoon winds as they had done for generations. The Indian population of Mombasa was descended from labour imported from India by the British in the early days of Colonialism to assist in the building of the Mombasa to Nairobi Railway. Presumably, the local African population at this time had not achieved the necessary skills for this work. No doubt, also, the majority of the British railway engineers and supervisors engaged for the project would have worked in India and would naturally been inclined to bring semi-skilled labour from that country. As traders and small shopkeepers, the Indian has few peers and their small shops or "dukas", as they were called, could be found virtually everywhere that people lived in the country.

We expatriates lived a pleasant life in spite of the climate. We had a Golf Club, a Tennis Club and a Swimming Club. Contrary to the opinion we often heard expressed at home, we did, however, work hard, as well as playing hard.

Engineering in developing countries does require a great deal more effort than in developed countries, as the back-up trained technicians are just not available and every project requires on-the-job training, which is not normally a requirement in developed countries. Furthermore, the climate is unkind to Europeans and one must constantly take precautions against heat and tropical diseases.

For myself, I found working in the Mombasa Province a fascinating experience. Since protective sea-works such as jetties, sea walls, groynes etc. did not fall into the main Branch categories of the Ministry, which were Roads, Buildings and Water Supplies; Sea-works became my responsibility as the Executive Engineer.

This involved me in many interesting safaris up and down the East Coast of Kenya, inspecting and arranging for repairs to sea structures and meeting with local administrators and village elders in respect of new structure requirements.

At the start of my tour in Mombasa, I was housed in a bachelor's mess, the top floor of which was reserved for expatriate civil servants and the ground floor for the expatriate officers of the Kenya Police. It was an excellent arrangement as far as I was concerned, since it allowed me to make bachelor friends very quickly and it had a nice small bar where civil servants and police could meet together over a drink in the evening.

The Mombasa Police Force, at that time, was a comparatively small unit and officer rank was still held by expatriates, some of them sent on attachment from U.K. Police Forces, others had served in the old Palestine Police Force and overall they represented a very experienced body of men. Their sergeants and constables (known in Kenya as "askaris") were a highly disciplined lot and representatives of several Kenya tribes could be found in their ranks

Frequently Mombasa would be "invaded" by sailors from a visiting ship, who, having tired of the delights of the Port bars and brothels, sallied forth into the main town looking for trouble and inevitably, fights would then ensue in the streets and local bars. When these got out of hand, we civilian bachelors were sometimes called on to assist the police and on such occasions being young and fit, we armed ourselves with pick handles and assisted the outnumbered police to separate the contestants, who were usually very drunk and could be abusive to the African askaris.

At one stage, during my time in Mombasa, I was asked by the Provincial Engineer to travel up north to the Coastal town of Malindi and build a jetty there for the benefit of the local fishermen. I went accompanied by a Building Superintendent, a foreman and a gang of labourers. To me, this was a very interesting project, as I had to carry out the design of the jetty myself. The site was in a beautiful part of the Coast with a lagoon formed by a coral reef outside and miles of sandy beach.

It also had the unusual attraction, that, as the construction proceeded seawards, and we did not have any pontoon equipment, at the stage when the foundation construction work passed beyond the high tide level, work could only be carried out when the tide had ebbed sufficiently. This meant that towards the end of the project, we only had time for two hours of work time between tides. The result of this was that we could legitimately spend a good deal of time goggle fishing and swimming inside the reef in ideal conditions in what was virtually a tropical paradise.

Such projects in civil engineering are a rarity!

Of course, as it is said, every tropical paradise has its down side, and the Malindi area was no exception. Malarial mosquitoes abounded and it was essential to take anti-malarial tablets and sleep under a mosquito net at night. I also found out, the hard way, that there is some kind of sea flea, which at certain times of the year attaches itself to floating pieces of seaweed, and if you touch this weed, you will get bitten all over, very painfully.

The Coastal area also produced a type of ground flea, known locally as a "jigger", which could burrow in between your toes or under your toe nail and lay its eggs there. You knew when this had happened to you if your toe began to itch and if the egg sac was not removed intact at this stage, your foot could rapidly become septic. Africans who went barefoot or with light sandals were well acquainted with these pests and were very expert at removing the egg sac with a blunt safety pin, so we Europeans usually asked our houseboys for their assistance to remove these unpleasant creatures and their eggs.

Another and even more unpleasant type of fly burrowed under your skin and laid its eggs there, usually on your arm or leg. The first you might know this had happened was when a small lump appeared at the site of the bite and shortly afterwards a most revolting large white maggot's head would pop out through the spot and have to be removed. I always thought that these maggot flies were the worst of the bugs, which afflicted us on the Coast.

For some reason, dogs were particularly prone to these maggots and many a time I had to remove them from my unfortunate pet.

The Ministry of Works Coastal Province covered an area inland for nearly 100 miles and this area, which was approached by driving up the main Mombasa to Nairobi road, gradually changed as you drove away from the lush coastal vegetation to the thorn trees and grasslands of the plains. Wildlife of all kinds abounded in both types of countryside and snakes were very much in evidence in the vicinity of the Coast. There was a particularly unpleasant type of snake that had the habit of living in mango trees and dropping down on you if you threw stones up the tree to knock down ripe mangoes. It was a very small green coloured snake, which I saw a few times and kept well away from, since it was reputed to be highly poisonous.

I found it strange that the local African population appeared to be unable to distinguish between poisonous and non-poisonous snakes. They apparently worked on the assumption that all snakes were poisonous and killed them indiscriminately. In one road camp on the

Nairobi road, where I sometimes lunched with the road foreman, the dry toilet, which was basically a deep hole in the ground covered with a home made toilet seat, was the favourite resting place of a family of hooded cobras. One approached the toilet with care and banged around the seat and surrounds with a stick before sitting down and I certainly did not delay during my visits!

I mentioned elephants on the Mombasa to Nairobi road before and I was to become very familiar with them during my time in Mombasa Province. One met elephant constantly on the main road and they could be a considerable nuisance as they strolled along the road tearing down branches to feed on the twigs and leaves and scattering the branches along the carriageway as they went. It was often necessary to get out of your car and clear the branches in order to proceed and frequently necessary to stop and wait for elephants to move off the road. They had a habit, sometimes, of making false charges at your car, which was very frightening, until you learnt that, they were only trying to scare you off and did not really mean you any harm.

Rhino were a particular problem at night since they liked to have dust baths in the sandy road surface and were difficult to see in the dark on a gravel road. Like other animals, they could become confused with vehicle headlights, but I am glad to say that I never actually hit one. If you did, your car would certainly be a write-off.

I did once see a car, which had hit a giraffe. As you may imagine, they could be particularly difficult to see at night, since they stood so tall that only their thin legs would be visible in the headlights. In this case, the unfortunate animal had his leg broken and fell on the car, kicking through the windscreen with another leg as he fell. The car was a write-off and the driver and passengers were lucky to escape with their lives.

Periodically, elephant herds came down to the Coast and laid waste large areas of valuable crops of maize and sugar cane belonging to local villagers. In these cases, the local Game Rangers tried with firecrackers and blank cartridges to drive them away. Sometimes, however, the number of elephant in the National Parks had reached numbers that were too great for the Park area to sustain and it became necessary to cull them before they moved in force into the populated coastal areas.

I happened one day to meet the Game Ranger who had been given the task of culling one of these herds that had descended on the Coastal farms. Like all the men in this service that I ever met, he loved his elephants and hated having to do this job, but it had to be done. We became quite friendly and he asked me if I would like to come on safari with him to see how culling was done.

Being young and interested in seeing everything that went on in Africa, I readily agreed and we left for the designated area with a team of Game Scouts, who, as I recall, were mostly armed in those days with .303 sporting rifles. In my ignorance, I had presumed that this type of elephant shooting was done from a reasonable distance away, but I was in for a shock to my system!

We found the elephant in heavy cover after tracking them for some two hours, the Game Ranger and his Scouts then stalked into the midst of the herd and elephant were picked out and shot at close range.

The ability of elephants to camouflage themselves in thick bush became immediately apparent to me, as I stood as close as I could to the Game Ranger! As the culling proceeded, elephant, that I had not seen until now, erupted from all around us and crashed off into the distance, whilst several of their number fell dead or dying from the expert shooting of the Game Staff. It was an experience, which I am not likely to forget in a hurry, and I was relieved to be able to get away from the bloody business of cutting out the ivory, which then had to take place.

In retrospect, I can appreciate that it was a necessary operation at the time and it was carried out with efficiency and minimum pain to the animals concerned, but I would not wish to see the spectacle repeated. It was the first time that I really understood the ability of elephants to move their enormous bulk noiselessly through thick cover and how difficult it can be to see them in such circumstances. In fact, on a later occasion, when stalking some buck to shoot for food for the survey party that I had with me, the only inkling I had that there were elephants near me, was when I heard the rumbling of an elephant's stomach very close by. I may say that I left as quickly and quietly as possible.

The destructive power of elephants can be quite incredible. There existed a beautiful spot, like an oasis in the desert, some many miles from Mombasa that was called Mzima Springs. Here, several springs of fresh, clear water bubbled up into several pools that abounded with small fish and was the source of drinking water for many herds of game for miles around, as well as being the home of several hippos.

At a time when Mombasa was expanding beyond the capabilities of its existing water supplies, the Ministry had decided it was necessary to tap the Mzima Springs in order to alleviate this problem. The project was a major undertaking at the time and involved laying a pipeline of very large diameter pipes (I forget the actual size) in a line from Mzima Springs to Mombasa. The pipes were cast in Mombasa using what was then a comparatively new system of concrete prestressed pipes. For ease of access, the pipeline followed a line parallel to the main road for many miles of its length. As happens in all pipelines, it was necessary to fit break pressure valves at intervals.

I was urgently contacted one morning and told that the main Mombasa Nairobi road was impassable over one section due to flooding. It transpired that an elephant herd, looking for water, had scented it at a valve on the pipeline and then proceeded to rip up the line at that point. The pipes adjoining the valve being prestressed had exploded under the stress of being pulled out of the ground and there was now a large pool, which incorporated part of the main road, where several happy elephants were disporting themselves in our lovely clean water.

One day my boss, the Provincial Engineer, suggested that I take a trip up the Coast to visit the District Commissioners at a place called Kipini at the mouth of the Tana River and go on from there to the island of Lamu where there was another District Headquarters.

My brief was to inspect the maintenance work, which had been carried out by the District Commissioners in these Districts. For this work, they were meant to use a small amount of the Ministry of Works building maintenance funds, which we allocated to them annually from our own meagre allocation. District Commissioners were both the Administrators and the Magistrates in their Districts. It was, I suppose, only natural that they tended to feel they could do what they liked with the maintenance funds issued to them. The Provincial Engineer had told me that it had been known for these funds to be expended in the past on building something, rather than for maintaining the existing Government structures. For this reason, he felt it necessary to carry out periodic inspections of the Government buildings in the more remote Districts. I suppose this might seem a minor item to those who have not worked in the Civil Service, but the P.E. could get into serious trouble with the Ministry Internal Audit Section if these funds were found to have been misallocated.

So, in due course, accompanied by an Inspector from the Buildings Branch, and in a Government Land Rover, I set forth for the town of Kipini. The North road at this time had several river estuary crossings that were too wide and therefore too expensive to have been bridged. These crossings were supplied with car ferries that were manned by M.O.W. crews who manually pulled the ferries across by a cable fixed to either bank. Africans loved to sing when doing hard manual work and the crews of these ferries were no exception.

As soon as the ferry was loaded, the crew leader would start the song and this would be accompanied by loud thumps of their feet as they moved along the length of the ferry pulling the cable. The content of these songs usually caused great mirth among the African passengers and I was told that the reason for this was that the words of the songs were made up at each crossing and always contained some passing reference to the passengers on board – particularly the Europeans! I would love to have known what they said about me but my knowledge of local dialects was not up to it.

Prior to our departure, telegrams had been despatched to the D.C.'s concerned giving approximate times of arrival. Lamu had replied, but, rather ominously, not even a second telegram to Kipini had produced any reply. I should explain that Kipini was one of the more remote Districts of that part of Kenya, a bachelor station for a District Commissioner whose District stretched up the valley of the Tana River and could only be traversed satisfactorily by camel safari.

The D.C.'s posted to these type of areas lived in almost complete isolation from other Europeans and in consequence some of them became, to say the least, became a little eccentric. I believe that it was very wrong to place these young bachelors in such remote places with heavy responsibilities for a whole two-year tour and expect them to remain normal human beings. At least some of them, I know, found it extremely difficult to return to normal civilised life after these periods and must have suffered serious problems in after life. As development of the Country proceeded, this situation was to improve considerably as other expatriate officers, such as Agricultural Officers, Police Inspectors and Veterinary Officers became a necessity for these areas and came to live in the same boma with these Administrators

To return to our trip to Kipini, the road we travelled was the main road to Lamu and ran inland parallel to the Coast. It was basically a sandy gravel surfaced road, which deteriorated into a sand track as we passed beyond the limits of heavy traffic usage. Anyway, we had plenty of experience of driving along this type of road surface in a Land Rover and we made good time, reaching the link road to Kipini in the late afternoon.

It was shortly after we turned down this road that we began to meet trees and branches blocking the thoroughfare. We stopped and removed them and drove on only to meet further similar obstacles. It began to dawn on us that these were not the usual results of passing elephant herds, but man-made obstructions, and we started to wonder what was in store for us at the end of the road.

We finally reached the end of the road and there in front of us was the District Commissioner's House and the Administration offices. Beyond them lay the beach and the sea and below them the fishing village of Kipini. We went in to the offices only to find that a court was in session and the presiding Magistrate, the D.C., was seated in his magisterial chair wearing only the type of sarong garment called a kikoi used by the local Coastal tribes.

I must say I thought his dress looked a little out of place, since he was accompanied by his tribal police askaris, who were, as usual with all uniformed Africans, very smartly turned out in spotless uniforms. The D.C. made little attempt to greet us, (a very unusual situation in these remote stations, where guests with white faces were usually very welcome) but sent an orderly with us to his house, which was right beside the office anyway. It was a fine large, double storied, square building of typical Colonial design with a corrugated iron roof. The second floor had a huge veranda, which went around all four sides of the building.

We were very travel-stained and weary at this stage, so we were pleased to eventually find the D.C.'s cook/houseboy. We were not so pleased to be told that he did not know that we were coming and no arrangements had been made for us, either in the line of food or bed accommodation. Wearily we returned to the Courthouse and this time found the D.C. in a more communicative mood. He finally admitted that he supposed he had received the telegrams, but appeared to assume that we had camp equipment with us, so he would not be involved. This was totally contrary to the normal practice on such occasions, when D.C.'s were expected to house and feed visiting Government Officers and I had to inform him of this expectation on our part, since we had minimal camping gear with us.

With some bad grace, he eventually sent for his houseboy and told him to make the necessary arrangements. We had showers and changed and feeling much better went in search of our host. When we found him, sitting on his upstairs veranda, he said that he hoped we had brought food with us, as he was preparing for a camel safari up river and ate only one banana per night for his evening meal! Once again, I went in search of his houseboy and persuaded him to go down to the village and buy us fish to make some kind of a meal. This transaction was successfully completed and we were eventually able to sit down at his dining table with the D.C. at the head with his one banana on a plate and the two of us with some very tasty fish.

After our meal, the atmosphere thawed somewhat, our reluctant host moved back to his chair on the veranda, and it now transpired that he might not be a great trencherman, but he certainly could put down his beer! One complete side of the veranda was in use as a storage area for crates of beer and it appeared that the D.C. had adopted a simple system of moving his chair to an area of full crates as others became empty. A pleasant evening now ensued as our host mellowed remarkably as the crates emptied and we gave him plenty of assistance in this project!

For some reason I had been allocated a large room on the ground floor and here I was destined to spend a very uncomfortable night. The room furniture consisted of my camp bed and not much else except an oil lamp sitting on a bedside table. The room itself opened directly onto the lower veranda and faced towards the beach and the sea. On the grass outside there were two old cannons and sited beside them small piles of cannon balls. I had heard nothing about the history of these cannon and mention them only because of the strange occurrences that befell me during that night.

I was very tired and quickly dropped off to sleep, lulled by the gentle murmur of the surf on the beach outside. I was suddenly awakened to hear strange noises outside. The noises were those of heavy objects, like cannon balls, being rolled along the veranda and were accompanied by the mutter of low voices. I found myself quite unable to move out of bed in order to light the lamp and find out what was going on. I suppose I was paralysed with fear of what I might find if I did go outside. The noises continued for some time and then gradually petered out and I dropped off to sleep again.

Waking up at dawn, as one tends to do in the tropics, I went out on the veranda and as far as I could see the cannon balls had not been moved, nor was there any sign of anything having taken place on the veranda. There was, however, a large python slithering down one of the pillars and I waited patiently for him to depart, which he duly did by disappearing under the floorboards.

Altogether, it had been an interesting night and I was relieved to find the Inspector of Works and proceed to the dining room. Here we found the District Commissioner moodily eating his banana ration, whilst his houseboy produced excellent fresh Mangoes and tiny fried local chicken eggs for the two of us.

After breakfast, our host took us for his morning walk, the object of which was apparently to view the graveyard situated on the sea front a short distance from his house. The graveyard contained the graves of some D.C.'s of the past and several missionaries, whose bodies had been brought down the Tana River from remote mission stations for burial in this station graveyard. It was sad to note, from the grave inscriptions, how very young most of these men were when they died. Presumably, their death in many cases resulted from malaria, yellow fever or other tropical diseases, which were not easily treatable in those days.

It seemed to us a not very healthy occupation for a young man like this D.C. to be so preoccupied, as he obviously was, with the graves of his predecessors. In fact, this unfortunate young man had eventually to be removed from his station and sent home on medical grounds. I went to see him in his hotel, in Mombasa, before he left for U.K. and he was obviously in poor mental health and finding it very difficult to adjust to civilisation again.

We duly completed our inspection of Government property in Kipini and proceeded up the Coast towards Lamu. I have little recollection of the mainland opposite Lamu Island, I am sure there must have been a village there, but it obviously made little impression on me at the time. Lamu Island, however, was a different story and I have vivid recollections of it. Our transport to the Island was by Arab dhow and this, in itself was an interesting experience. Arab dhows of all shapes and sizes had plied their trade up and down the Coast of Africa and across to the Middle East for generations and it was interesting to sail in one, even for such a short trip. I cannot say that they were very comfortable, but they were practical and did the job, provided the wind was favourable.

At that time, Arabs and African descendants of slaves (who would have been captured inland in the days when the slave trade flourished) inhabited Lamu Island. I believe it is true to say that, in those days, the Arabs were the main slave dealers on this Coast of Africa. I found Lamu a most fascinating place. A true old Arab Town had changed little for centuries. No mechanical transport was allowed on the Island, at that time and donkeys performed the duties of personal transport as well as being the beasts of burden. The narrow winding streets divided houses, which were often three stories high, many with elaborately carved doors. In the few where one could see inside there was a large open courtyard with rooms built around tiers of balconies.

We stayed in what was then the only hotel on Lamu Island, the famous Petley's Hotel. I gathered Petley had been a white hunter in his younger days and although now a fairly old man, he still kept a strict eye on his Arab staff and the Hotel, such as it was, operated quite smoothly. I say, "such as it was", because the bedrooms had no doors and were partitioned only by curtains that served as doors and walls and privacy was virtually non-existent. I found it fascinating to listen to the old man and his stories of Coastal Kenya in the old days. At some time a leopard had mauled him and he still suffered a good deal from the old claw wounds. I had always heard that being clawed by a leopard caused serious septicaemia, since their claws were full of unpleasant bacteria due to their habit of eating their kills in a putrescent state, and here was living proof of that fact.

Perhaps the most famous of the facilities of Petley's Hotel were the "long drop" toilets. As far as I could see these were sited at the edge of a deep circular structure, adjoining the hotel and extending for the full height of the building. The toilet cubicles were built into this structure at each floor level. This effectively allowed human waste from all these cubicles to fall and be deposited in one large hole, presumably situated below ground level. No wonder Petley's dry toilets were famous in that part of the world!

After a couple of days spent inspecting Government buildings in Lamu District with a very helpful District Commissioner, we re-crossed the sea to the mainland, collected our Land Rover and started back on the road to Mombasa. On the way, we stopped off at Malindi, (a Coastal village which was fast developing into a Tourist Resort with a nice small hotel), where we had some Government buildings to inspect and then returned to our Headquarters.

About this time, life in Mombasa for me began to make some dramatic changes. I decided that I was a fed up with life in the bachelor's mess and was lucky enough to obtain accommodation in a Government rented flat, which gave me more freedom of movement. I acquired a houseboy, a tall well-built Jaluo tribesman called David whose people came from the hot plains around Lake Victoria. David was a most cheerful soul who always was in good humour and was a reasonable cook and an excellent houseboy. I can still recall an incident, which perhaps typified his outlook on life.

I was in my flat, finishing a report on some work and David was ironing in the kitchen. Suddenly there was an almighty crash from the kitchen. I ran in, to find David standing, looking at the electric iron, which was lying on the floor. I asked him what had happened.

He replied in Swahili that the iron was "mbaya", a Swahili word which means "bad".

I said in Swahili "why, what is wrong with it?" and picked up the iron. Immediately I received a heavy electric shock, which made me drop the iron with a crash on the floor.

David looked at me with his broad grin and said, "You see Bwana, that is exactly what happened to me!"

One night I went for a drink in the bachelor's mess and one of the Police Inspectors said to me :

"You must go out to White Sands Hotel, Trevor and meet the smashing Irish girl who is working out there." So, I did, and so she was, and so I met an Irish girl from Wicklow, who in due course, consented to become my wife and we were married in Mombasa and have lived together happily ever since.

Mombasa had a good social life for married expatriates with the facilities of several coastal hotels with beautiful beaches not far away, an interesting golf course and at least two other Clubs. We were lucky enough to be eventually allocated a nice Government House. We managed to acquire good house servants, which helped my wife to deal with the extreme climatic conditions, conditions that made cooking and housework very difficult for European women.

The golf course, due to climatic conditions, was particularly unusual. It was not possible to grow grass suitable for greens, so these were made of sand, which was raked, into shape after every usage. Tees were constructed from tarmac, which meant that conventional golf tees could not be used for teeing up the balls, as the surface was impenetrable. As a beginner at Golf, I suppose Mombasa Golf Course was a tough place to learn the game. I recall two holes in particular, which cost me a lot of money in golf balls!

From the tee on one of these holes you had to drive across a sea inlet and if you did not make it, your ball ended up in the sea. The other hole was even more interesting. Here the tee was situated on a high spot overlooking the beach with a main road running below you and the fairway ran parallel to the road, but at a considerable height above it. Any slight miscalculation, such as a slice, meant that the ball almost certainly landed somewhere on the tarmac road below and bounced along the road and either ended up hitting a car or disappearing onto the beach below. For a beginner at the game, these two holes were a nightmare, since, as anyone who has become involved in the early stages of this infuriating game would know, the harder you try to avoid an obstacle, the more likely you are to end up in the middle of it!

The Mombasa Swimming Club had its own interesting features. The swimming area was situated in a section of a creek, which ran up from the main harbour, and it was protected from possible shark problems by a net surround. Some distance upstream of the Club was the town abattoir. It appeared that when the abattoir was operational, some blood and offal entered the creek. The local sharks naturally scented this and schools of them rushed up the creek to join in this free banquet. If you were unfortunate enough to be swimming at that time, you would suddenly see lines of shark fins passing just outside the safety net, a nerve-wracking sight which I, for one, did not wait to admire on these occasions.

Goggle fishing in the many lagoons inside the reefs at various places along the coast was a popular pastime and one I always enjoyed. One could hire an outrigger canoe, be paddled out to the inner edge of the reef and goggle fish there to your heart's content. These days you can see all these extraordinary fish in their beautiful colours on television any time, but in those days, they were a novelty, which we were privileged to enjoy. I also used to carry a harpoon gun and try to shoot some of the larger specimens for eating. It took time to realise that what looked like an edible sized fish through underwater goggles, could turn out to be sprat sized when harpooned and brought to the surface.

The water in the lagoons was incredibly clear and the variety of fish and their colours was wonderful to see. Mind you, there were also some poisonous sea snakes around, but I do not recall hearing of anyone being bitten by one. My wife used to join me on these expeditions, until one day when we were goggling inside a reef and came to the surface to locate our canoe, we saw the fin of a shark not far away and inside the reef. This was a very unusual sight as sharks did not come inside the reef as a rule, but it marked the end of my dear wife's goggling expeditions! In fact, if the truth were known, it was a very small shark and was probably trying to find its way out of the lagoon.

Our tour in Mombasa ended and we went on home leave and spent a happy three months touring around Ireland and meeting up with friends and relations.

CHAPTER 9
NAIROBI DAYS

The home leave system, as practised at that time, made it almost a necessity for junior officers, to be moved to a different station on return from their leave, since it was not very practical to hold their post unoccupied for three months.

It was, therefore, no great surprise to find, on my return, that I was posted to Nairobi Provincial Headquarters as Assistant to the Provincial Road Engineer.

In this position I was involved in the construction of a new road through the coffee growing area of Kiambu, where my particular responsibility related to designing and supervising the construction of two reinforced concrete bridges and several reinforced concrete box culverts. I also learnt, (unofficially!) how to operate bulldozers and scrapers, thanks to a friendly South African Road Superintendent. I learnt how roads were constructed in what was called "black cotton soil", a very heavy black clay with organic content which was like a rock when dry, but like a skating rink when wet. The only practical way to deal with this soil was to dig it out (and it was sometimes six foot deep) and backfill with imported material, a very expensive road building exercise. As I found out later, this type of clay soil occurred in many different areas of Kenya, and many miles of new road that had to be built using this expensive methodology.

Nairobi was a pleasant station for us. We were allocated a nice Government House and had many friends of our own age, so we had a good social life. The climate was good, not too hot and sticky like Mombasa and it was possible to have a nice garden, as the soil was fertile and rainfall reasonable. I played tennis and hockey, both of these games were played on gravel surfaces that could give you a nasty cut if you slipped and fell. I also took up rugby again which I had not played since leaving College, so I was probably fitter at this time than I ever have been, before or since.

Our first son was born whilst we were in Nairobi and turned out to be a model baby who gave us the minimum of problems and thrived in the climate. This was a time when road development in Kenya was proceeding apace and it was soon possible to drive up country on smooth bitumen surfaced main roads, instead of rattling along the corrugated gravel surfaces to which we had become accustomed.

Nearly two years passed and we found ourselves on the move again, posted this time as Provincial Road Engineer to the town of Kisumu in Nyanza Province. Kisumu was situated on Lake Victoria not far from the Uganda border and nearly as far west as one could go in Kenya. It was a small town serving the lake fishermen and local farmers and was a very different story to Mombasa or Nairobi, as the expatriate population consisted, mainly, of Government Officers, like ourselves. Here, in the sticky heat of a Kisumu dry season, was born our daughter, who turned out to be a very different child to our first-born. She was an exceptionally active child who, unlike her brother, needed little sleep and made sure that we were kept in the same situation!

We settled happily into this small, friendly community. There was the usual Club with golf course, tennis courts, squash court and swimming pool where all the expatriates gathered on a weekend and, of course, the great expanse of Lake Victoria was right beside us. The climate was hot and humid and not unlike Mombasa, and we had spectacular thunderstorms in the rainy season, which started out on the Lake and roared in over the Town, usually knocking out the electricity and making the telephone jump off its stand with sparks flying out of it.

We kept well away from the windows on these occasions, as the roof was of corrugated iron and every sheet was earthed to a plate in the garden. The result of this was that, if the roof was struck by fork lightning, (which happened not infrequently) the lightning was diverted to earth in the garden beside the house. This could be a frightening sight if you were standing near a window.

Lake Victoria abounded in fish, crocodiles, hippos, and the hippos came ashore at night to graze and frequently wandered across the golf course, where their large feet left deep imprints in the fairways. These were listed as "Hazards" in the Club Rules, a rule that used to cause some amusement to visitors, but it was a genuine requirement in the circumstances.

Hippos can be dangerous animals, especially if they have young, and it was by no means unusual to hear that they had overturned a fisherman's canoe, or sometimes chopped one in half and seriously injured the occupants. They were also very noisy animals and you could hear their snorts and bellows from a long distance away, particularly towards nightfall. It was very pleasant in the cool of the evening to stroll along the edge of the Lake and see the schools of hippo moving around in the water. One could not stay too long, however, as dusk brought the bugs out in force and Kisumu was a bad area for malaria mosquitoes.

One weekend, I thought it would be interesting to try fishing for tilapia in the Lake. I was advised that a piece of raw meat would be good bait, so my wife and I duly arrived at the lakeshore armed with a spinning rod and the necessary bait. After a few casts that brought no results, I handed the rod to my wife for her to have a try. Almost immediately the float sank out of sight and a long underwater battle took place with what, I presumed, was a very large fish of some kind. To our astonishment, the "fish" turned out to be a large freshwater tortoise, which eventually came to the surface, swam ashore, walked up the bank, and gave itself up with the hook hanging out of its mouth! Needless to say, this was the last time that I was able to persuade my wife to go fishing in Lake Victoria.

The rice fields that were cultivated in the area around Lake Victoria provided great feeding for various varieties of wild geese and duck and the Assistant Commissioner of Police, the Provincial Medical Officer (another Irishman) and I had several successful shooting evenings in these rice fields. We were aware of the danger of contracting the unpleasant disease of bilharzia whilst wading, as we did, in shorts and tennis shoes in these fields. We were, however, informed that the snail that carried this unpleasant bug existed only in the more stagnant, weedy parts of the waterways, so we kept away from these areas. I suppose the fact that we had a doctor with us also added to our confidence!

On one famous occasion we were caught in a
ferocious rainstorm and, on return to our vehicle found,
that the road was now impassible at a stream crossing.
We had no alternative but to approach the chief of a
nearby village and ask for accommodation for the night.
This was readily made available and we were fed on
fried eggs and allocated a hut for the night that
contained one large bed. Here the Medical Officer and
myself settled down to try and sleep, but we had not
anticipated the onslaught of voracious bed bugs which
attacked us and made sleep nearly impossible. The next
morning the stream had subsided sufficiently to allow
us to return to Kisumu, where we were greeted by two
very worried wives.

On some weekends, in order to get a respite
from the heat and humidity of Kisumu, we used to
drive up to the hills above the plains surrounding Lake
Victoria, to one of the tea growing areas of Kenya. Here
there was a small town called Kericho, which had a
hotel and club, which catered for the tea planter
community. Kericho was cool and pleasant, but it
appeared to rain every afternoon, a soft drenching rain.
This weather pattern, no doubt, was the reason why the
tea bushes grew so well, but not so good for those who
lived there and had to work during the day, as it
curtailed any outdoor activity after work. Anyway, to us
it was a pleasant change of climate and, sometimes, we
stayed over the weekend and revelled in the cool nights.

In the course of time, the Provincial Engineer
went on home leave and I took over as Acting Provincial
Engineer. Soon after this I was summoned one morning
to the Provincial Commissioner's Office, to be told that
Kisumu was to be honoured with a visit from Princess

Margaret. I cannot think why it had been decided for her to visit such a small Provincial Station, but I am sure that the Governor had some good reason for the arrangement. Anyway, the proposed visit put the P.C. in a great flap and we were inundated with urgent instructions and practice parades. I remember that I had to buy a felt hat for the occasion, since I did not possess any thing other than a khaki safari hat at the time.

The Ministry of Works became heavily involved in resurfacing the Airport tarmac area where the Princess was to alight from the plane and yards of barriers had to be constructed to assist the Police in crowd control. We then marked the newly surfaced tarmac area with innumerable dots and white lines to delineate where everyone was to stand to meet the lady in question. The local Kenya Police Band and King's African Rifles Guard of Honour were drilled and drilled again on their positions and actions in relation to the newly painted white lines.

The great day duly arrived and we all took up our designated positions. The 'plane landed and the pilot taxied in to his appointed spot while the band struck up the National Anthem in what one could only describe as their own inimitable African way!

We waited. The plane started up again and turned around facing the opposite direction and the Princess descended on the far side, throwing all the Provincial Commissioner's wonderful arrangements into some confusion, as everyone was now on the side of the plane away from the landing party. Somehow, the situation was sorted out and the royal party left for the Provincial Commissioner's house where the princess was to tidy up and then proceed to the Town Hall for a formal luncheon. In the event, this did not happen, as the Princess apparently said she was not fit to attend the function. So ended a disastrous day for a number of persons who had done a great deal of work for this occasion.

We found out later the Princess had told the pilot she would not alight on the appointed side of the plane, as the tarmac was too rough, so he had to turn the plane around. It was also rumoured that she had simply refused point blank to attend the formal luncheon. If these stories were correct, then she certainly had little respect for those who had done their best to make the day a success.

CHAPTER 10.
I VISIT THE NORTHERN DESERTS

Once again, we reached the end of another tour of duty, packed up house and flew home on vacation leave. This leave was the first one we had with two children to show off to their respective grandparents. We also found time to stay in a flat in the old Rectory in Ardmore, Co. Waterford, which belonged to an aunt of mine, and I was able to get in some pheasant and duck shooting in the area.

On our return to Kenya, I was posted as Provincial Road Engineer to the Provincial Headquarters of Nyeri Province situated in the Highlands of Kenya in the Tribal area of the Kikuyu Tribe. Nyeri was another 'plum' Station as far as the Ministry of Works was involved as the town was situated at a high altitude with a cool climate that required open fires at night during some times of the year. The surroundings were forest and good agricultural land, which was populated by Kikuyu farmers.

There was a very pleasant Club situated on the edge of an excellent golf course with real grass for the fairways, instead of the brown tufts we had become accustomed to elsewhere. The real bonus, as far as I was concerned, was that there was fairly good trout fishing in the streams around which descended from the slopes of Mount Kenya. Mount Kenya itself was not too far away, and its peaks could be seen on a clear day. Of course, there had to be drawbacks to the climate at this attitude. During the rainy season, we had many days when the whole area was covered in mist for the day, but to anyone coming from Ireland, this was not exactly a new phenomenon!

Anyone who is unfamiliar with the Geography of Kenya would probably not realise that a large part of the northern part of Northern Kenya is virtually a desert area. Here rainfall is negligible and intermittent, and the country is scattered with nomad tribes depending on sheep, goats and camels for their living. The designated boundary of the Ministry of Works Province of Nyanza incorporated a large slice of this country, which was administratively referred to as the 'Northern Province of Kenya'.

As Provincial Road Engineer, I was responsible for the maintenance of some hundreds of miles of road that existed in this desert area and in some places reached the borders of Somalia. It was perhaps a bit complimentary to call them 'Roads', as they were, in the main sandy tracks that, at intervals, crossed dry riverbeds using concrete slabs over concrete pipes and were called 'drifts'. These waterways could become major rivers if and when there was heavy rainfall in the vicinity and were frequently washed away by the force of water and vegetation being hurled down by the floods. Funding for the maintenance of these roads was very meagre due to the negligible wheeled traffic and it was a constant battle, not only to maintain the roads, but also to keep maintenance staff in this part of the world.

I had not been long in Nyeri, before it became necessary for me to take a trip into this Northern Frontier Province (known everywhere in Kenya as the N.F.P.) to inspect the roads and meet our one and only Road Foreman, who lived a nomad existence in this area in a caravan supplied by the Ministry. His Unit consisted of a maintenance road grader with operator; two tipper lorries with drivers and a gang of labourers all of whom lived in Government supplied tents. With this outfit he did his best to keep somewhere about two hundred miles of road in passable order.

Naturally, such a lonely existence would not suit many expatriates, particularly as he seldom saw fresh fruit or vegetables and had to exist on a diet of goat meat obtained from the local tribesmen. The person, who occupied this post, when I first took over the roads in the Province, was an Englishman who seemed peculiarly suited to this unusual lifestyle. His history was a mystery to us, but he was certainly an educated man and rumour had it that he was descended from the Aristocracy and was what was known in those days as a 'Remittance Man'. This was apparently defined as someone from an aristocratic family in U.K. who was paid to stay away from home by his family, as a penance for some deed he had committed in his past!

I have no idea whether this story was true or not, but I do know that he was an exemplary Road Foreman, who was conscientious and hard working and his hobby was classical music. The music, in records, was carried in a small trailer, which was towed behind his lorry from camp to camp and in the course of time; I spent several pleasant evenings, sitting in the veranda of his tent listening to his records.

As I recall, there were two main destinations for these arterial roads. One branch went to the Border with Somalia at a place called Wajir and the other ended in a place called Moyale on the Border with Ethiopia. Wajir was a District Commissioner's Station that I visited on several occasions. It had several expatriate officers. Besides the D.C. himself, there was a Police Superintendent, a Veterinary Officer and a platoon of the Kings African Rifles with their officer. Being on the border with Somalia meant that there were continual raids by local Somali tribesmen into Kenya and there were apparently many squabbles between the local Somali tribesmen over grazing and water, so the Army and Police were kept busy.

The N.F.P. Police Force was a crack paramilitary unit, armed with Lee Enfield Rifles and they wore khaki cotton hats with a protective neck flap reminiscent of the French Foreign Legion. They represented a force not to be argued with since most of their constables were recruited from the more belligerent warrior tribes of Kenya. Wajir station was constructed as a fort, brilliant white in colour, reminiscent of what one saw in the old French Foreign Legion films like Beau Geste, and it certainly fitted beautifully into the environment of the surrounding desert.

The District Commissioner, at the time, was a young bachelor Englishman, who seemed to have been able to adapt better than some to his circumstances, but, of course, he had several expatriates for company, unlike his opposite number in Kipini.

Marsabit, on the road to Moyale was situated in a totally different type of environment. It was an old volcanic intrusion, which stuck up out of the desert for some hundreds of feet, and the volcanic soils surrounding its sides and the deep crater were very fertile. This resulted in a mountainside and conical crater valley covered with a heavy growth of trees and bushes and produced a pleasant, relatively cool situation, well above the hot desert country below.

Game abounded round the mountain, including some herds of elephant. The area had been gazetted as a Game Reserve and an expatriate Game Warden lived there. It was quite fascinating to look down into this deep volcanic crater, which contained a small lake and see elephants walking around, way below you in the depths of the crater. The Game Warden of this area at the time was Terence Adamson, a brother of George Adamson, who was later to become famous for his work with Kenya lions.

Safaris in the N.F.P. by Government Officers on duty were carried out in some style! To inspect the total length of road maintained to the borders of Kenya in my Provincial area required a two-day safari up to the Border and a further two-day safari back to base. The day before my departure, a M.O.W. lorry would arrive at my house already loaded with all necessary camp equipment for the driver and myself. Then the lorry would take on board our 'garden boy' (who, in fact, was a houseboy in training) and all the cooking utensils and foodstuffs that my houseboy and my wife considered necessary.

The lorry would then depart for the first night campsite. The following morning, my driver with the Land Rover would arrive and I would climb on board with all required office equipment for the road inspection and we would take off for the trip. At the end of the day we would arrive travel-stained, weary and covered in dust from head to foot, to find our camp set up near a small oasis, hot water ready for a bath, bed made, beer on the table and food in preparation.

Very often, I would bring a shotgun with me and we would have shot a few francolins (a type of bush partridge) or guinea fowls on the way to add to the food supplies. Shortly before dusk, I might take my gun and wander down to the waterhole where large flocks of sand grouse would arrive to drink just before dark and if I were lucky, some of these would be added to the evening meal for the whole party.

Usually I would purchase a couple of fat tailed sheep from tribesmen on the return journey and these would be divided between the members of our staff and us. These N.F.P. sheep were a breed that carried their fat in their tails, like the hump of a camel. In spite of the harsh climate where they lived, these sheep produced excellent tender meat and they could be purchased at a very reasonable price in the desert areas. The unfortunate sheep would then be tethered by a long rope to graze on our lawn for a few days before being slaughtered. If you were not careful, when walking in the garden, the tethered sheep could provide some entertainment for members of the family, as they were expert at creeping up behind you and butting you up the bottom!

Both my wife and I returned to playing golf whilst in Nyeri and it was nice to play on such a well-kept course. We were also able to go on very pleasant weekend picnics in the surrounding forest area and it was not long before I found that these picnics could be combined with my passion for trout fishing. I found and explored in the forest area some lovely small, clear streams, which had been stocked with rainbow trout, and they gave me good sport. On one, not to be forgotten occasion, whilst fishing a small stream with banks heavily covered in vegetation, I was startled to hear a snort on the opposite bank, and looked up to see the enormous face of a buffalo gazing at me through the undergrowth. Knowing the aggressive reputation of these animals, I did not wait around, but beat a hasty retreat to my car!

During the rainy season, the gravel roads of the Province (which, in effect, incorporated all the roads outside townships) could become extremely slippery and difficult to negotiate except in four-wheel drive vehicles. In particular, the roads traversing the slopes of Mount Kenya, that were crossed at frequent intervals by streams emanating from the mountain snows, frequently became impassible. This was largely due to the fact that there were insufficient construction funds available to build the necessary bridges and water crossing largely consisted of 'drifts' i.e. concrete slabs laid over pipes. These were fine in dry weather, but rapidly became impossible to cross after heavy rain, as the water depth exceeded that which was safe to pass with a vehicle.

Road Engineers were expected to use their own vehicles and paid a mileage allowance, but few of us could afford the luxury of a Land Rover, which was the only easily available four-wheel drive vehicle in Kenya at that time. As a result, we became, of necessity, quite expert drivers on wet and slippery roads. On one occasion that I am unlikely to ever forget, I was sitting in my car at a drift crossing, many miles from home, contemplating the roaring flood in front of me, when a cheerful African driver in a Government Land Rover arrived. He examined the flooded drift and decided that, with his high clearance and four-wheel drive he

Plate 1

Samburu Nomads Camp in
Northern Frontier Province of Kenya

Plate 2

Somali Nomads moving house.
Their tent frames are loaded upside down on the camels

Plate 3

Camp in the Northern Frontier
Province of Kenya

Plate 4

Wajir Fort
Near the borders of Somalia

would chance it and he successfully made the crossing. At this stage the flood showed signs of abating, so he drove back across and offered to tow me over. With some misgivings I agreed to his offer and he attached a tow rope and off we went.

We were half way across the drift when, to my horror, my car started to float away downstream! I must say that the car remained remarkably buoyant and little water entered the cab, (probably because all our cars were very well dust-proofed due to the problems of dry weather driving on gravel roads) but I was, by now, well downstream of the drift and at an awkward angle to the tow vehicle. In fairness to the Land Rover driver, he did not lose his nerve, but continued to drive on up the road and my car was slowly pulled back on to dry land. Thankfully, I dried out the engine as best I could, rewarded my saviour, and headed for home.

The time came for the Provincial Engineer to go on vacation leave, and once again, I found myself Acting Provincial Engineer. In this position, one became responsible for the whole Provincial Ministry of Works set up, which included Government Buildings, Water Supplies and Roads. With an overall staff of some hundreds, one rapidly became more of an Administrative Manager than a technical Engineer and had to rapidly learn the necessary skills the hard way (something not taught in University in my day).

A very pleasant and competent young Polish engineer with a wife and young family then filled my post of Provincial Road Engineer and we became good friends. A visit to his Government allocated house involved a Polish ritual with which we were to become quite familiar. When you arrived, our host appeared with a tray containing small glasses of neat vodka which one was required to swallow down in one gulp. A fascinating custom, which certainly ensured a good start to the evening!

Independence was approaching rapidly in Kenya and more and more locals were acquiring the necessary professional qualifications to take over as Engineers in the various Branches. The problem was to get them the necessary practical experience in the short time now left to us.

As it transpired, this could not have happen in the available time, and after Independence, it was left in many cases to Aid-Funded Consultants to fulfil this role on a short-term basis. Not a very satisfactory solution, but the only alternative in the circumstances.

None of us in the Colonial Engineering Service should have had any illusions other than that, it was, and had always been our job to train locals to take over the professionals' posts from us as soon as they were experienced enough to do so. I certainly always felt this way, but for those expatriates, born in the country, whose parents and in some cases grandparents had worked to make Kenya what it had become, Independence was a bitter pill to swallow.

After Independence, many of the serving Colonial Service Officers, like myself, had to make the decision to stay on in Kenya on local contracts, or take our pensionable rights and leave.

In the end, we made the decision to leave Kenya for two reasons. The first was that I knew, sooner or later, I would have to get another job in civil engineering and if I did not make the effort at this time I would lose any contacts which I had in Ireland which could assist me in doing so. The second reason was that we felt that our children should be educated in Ireland and we did not want them to end up as boarders in schools with their parent's abroad. This was something that had happened to me when I was young and my parents were in Ceylon and I do not believe that it is the best way for children to grow up.

After fourteen happy years working in Kenya and the prospect of remaining there, if I so wished, to work with the Independent Government, it was a tough decision to make, but one that, I personally, have never regretted. Too often, we had seen and have seen many times since, the effects of this type of expatriate life on the children of our friends and colleagues. The continual worry of your children growing up without you being there for parental control and advice is not a satisfactory situation and should be avoided if at all possible.

CHAPTER 11.
WE LEAVE KENYA

So, we packed our bags, said farewell to our many friends and colleagues and returned to Ireland.

We decided that my old home area of Monkstown, Co. Dublin was in too built up an area for us after the open spaces of Africa, so we bought a house in Greystones, Co. Wicklow. Quite by chance, I obtained a temporary post as an Assistant County Engineer with Wicklow County Council and we placed the children in Schools and started our new life. After a year, I began to find engineering in Wicklow County Council was not a very exciting prospect and I obtained a post of Contractor's Agent with a well-known International Civil Engineering Contractors firm, The Cementation Company.

I worked with this Company on the construction of the Gouldings Factory in the East Wall in Dublin, where we were heavily involved in underground piling and a prestressed concrete water tank and several prestressed concrete grain silos. Subsequently I went to Omagh, Co. Tyrone in Northern Ireland with this Company to build a prestressed concrete bridge and motorway through Omagh Town. I have nothing but good to say about my time working with the Cementation Company. They were a highly professional organisation, which treated their staff extremely well.

Unfortunately, at the end of this period, they had no further work available in the Republic of Ireland and wanted me to take over as Manager in Northern Ireland, but this job I did not wish to undertake, so we parted on good terms.

I then obtained a post as Projects Manager with the Contracting firm of O'Connor and Bailey, who had been awarded the contract for the new Radio Studios for R.T.E. (the Irish Radio and Television Company) in Montrose, Co.Dublin. This was an interesting civil engineering project; since most of the studios were constructed, deep underground and we had to deal with considerable water pressure against the outer concrete walls. The studios were constructed as concrete walled rooms within an outer waterproof reinforced concrete skin. The building being below ground and the studios being sound insulated from the outer shell of the building was all part of the design to minimise external sound problems as conceived by the Architect Michael Scott.

After the completion of this contract, I continued to work for O'Connor and Bailey for some years as Major Projects Manager and was involved in many interesting office and apartment construction projects in Dublin City.

One day my eye was caught by an advertisement in the Irish Times paper regarding a job as Engineer to the Inland Fisheries Trust. For many years, I had been a Member of the Inland Fisheries Trust, which was a Semi-State Organisation dedicated to maintaining and improving the game fisheries of Ireland, and I had followed the records of its work in the Shannon and the other great trout fishing lakes of Ireland with interest. I had been a dedicated trout fisherman from the age of ten years and the thought of being involved in fishery engineering work was very attractive to me, so I posted off an application for the job.

Thus began five years of working in one of the best jobs I was ever lucky enough to attain.

Working in a small dedicated organisation with biologists and fishery staff who knew what they had to do and carried it out in all kinds of weather conditions was a very pleasurable occupation for me and I learnt a great deal about trout and salmon in this time. My job involved travelling to many lakes and rivers in Ireland, designing river improvements, taking water inflow measurements and being responsible for pollution control in Trust waters and I was very happy in my work.

Unfortunately, this situation ended when the Government decided that the Inland Fisheries Trust should be incorporated into the Department of Fisheries. I did not feel that I would be happy as a Civil Servant, so I tendered my resignation from this post.

Fortunately for me, the Irish Government decided just about this time that they would become involved in technical aid to the Southern African State of Lesotho, and I was asked to head a team of Road Engineers to assist the Ministry of Works in Lesotho in order to develop its road system.

We now had a second son who had been born in Ireland and inherited a tendency to have chest problems, so we thought that a change of climate to a hotter, drier environment might benefit him. Our two older children were now well advanced in their education and so we decided to take the chance of a return to Africa, taking our younger son with us.

CHAPTER 12
BACK TO AFRICA

Lesotho turned out to be a very different type of African climate and situation to that which we had become accustomed in Kenya. The old British name for Lesotho had been Basutoland and it would seem that, in its earlier days, it's chief claim to fame was its ponies. These small animals had adapted to the mountainous countryside so well that they appeared to be able to climb up inclines and over rocky outcrops carrying heavy loads, in what, I would imagine, was the type of terrain that mules would be used for in other countries. The Basotho were also known for their decorative blankets and conical shaped hats. Most villages had their own design of blanket and when they came to attend meetings in their rural areas, they presented a most colourful sight, riding in on their small ponies wearing their blankets and headgear.

In fact on the few occasions when, whilst on road inspections, I visited one of their villages, set high in the mountains, the local shops and beer dens resembled something from a Western film, with ponies tied to the rails outside these establishments. Their ponies were always most handsomely decorated with good leather harness and saddlery. They loved their ponies and really looked after them.

The small country of Lesotho was, in reality, a mountain range, to which some African tribesmen had fled in order to escape from the encroaching Boer Settler farmers, who had settled the lowlands around the Mountains, on lands that initially belonged to these tribes. In the course of time, the various tribesmen had joined together and elected a King and thereafter became the Basotho people.

The King had then appealed to Queen Victoria for protection from the Boers and she had sent a regiment all the way up from the Cape to assist the King in setting up his new country. This was apparently the history of how Lesotho emerged as an Independent Nation surrounded eventually by the Union of South Africa, but not part of it.

Such a nation, living on mountains at altitudes up to ten thousand feet, found it hard to eke out a living with a growing population and poor agricultural soil. It was inevitable, therefore, that a great proportion of the younger male population crossed the border into South Africa, where they obtained work in the mines. African miners in South Africa were relatively highly paid, so most of the prosperity of Lesotho emanated from the emigrant population, and it was noticeable that an unusual proportion of the employees in Lesotho were women, the men being away in South Africa.

We spent four good years in Lesotho. Our younger son went to the International School in Maseru (the Capital City of Lesotho). He did well there and his health greatly improved in the dry mountain climate, and by the time we returned to Ireland, he had successfully passed the International equivalent of the Irish Intermediate Certificate.

Unlike Kenya, which is on the Equator, Lesotho is a long way south and has a definite summer and winter climate. Rainfall occurs mostly in the summer period and the winters are dry and very cold until the sun is well up in the sky. In the Capital city of Maseru, where we were based, morning temperatures in the winter could be eight degrees of frost and this was in the lower part of the country! At eight thousand feet, there was permanent frost all year in the valleys where the sun did not reach and the winter brought heavy snowfalls. The mountain roads were frequently closed with snowdrifts and we used motor graders and small bulldozers as snowploughs to try and re-open them.

As I have already indicated, the Basotho people used their ponies as transport to those many places on the mountains where no roads existed and their villages were dotted anywhere that fertile soil could be found. Our job was to try and make a proper road network in this difficult terrain, in order that the villagers could bring their produce to market in the lowland areas, and having made the network, to set up a proper maintenance system to keep it in place. The country was small, probably no larger than Northern Ireland in size, but the terrain raised major engineering problems. The projected traffic on many of the mountain roads was too small to justify bitumen or tar surfaces, so suitable gravel had to be found and gradients minimised to stop gravel erosion in wet weather. This all made for interesting road engineering work.

I must admit that I was constantly impressed by the ability of the young Irish Engineers who were sent out to us in Lesotho, to adapt to these engineering conditions, which were so totally different to those to which they were accustomed. Local Civil Engineers were being trained in the U.S.A. and Britain and having qualified, were returning to their country during this period. Unfortunately, some of them did not stay for long, as South Africa was desperately trying to recruit

African Engineers at this time and the salary and conditions they were able to offer for black engineers were far better in that country.

Lesotho's climate was particularly suitable for growing fruit like peaches and apricots and we had a very prolific grapevine in our garden, as well as a plum tree. In the spring, the countryside would be dotted with fruit tree blossom – a rather unusual sight in mountainous country where other trees were virtually non-existent except in the lower valleys.

As far as expatriates pastimes were concerned, there were the usual Clubs where one could play tennis or golf. Accompanied by my younger son, I was soon able to sample the local fishing and we had some good sport on several occasions in local dams that had been stocked with large mouth bass. These hard fighting fish, and their firm, white flesh proved to be excellent eating. On a few occasions in the summer, we drove up into the mountains and stayed in a small hotel where we had some pleasant fishing for rainbow trout that the British had originally stocked in the streams at this high altitude. The road up to this mountain area was gravel surfaced for most of its length, and had sections of extremely high gradients combined with hairpin bends that made for interesting driving. The fact that vehicle wheels tended to lose their grip on the gravel on these high gradients and the hairpin bends did not help matters. Four-wheel drive vehicles were almost essential for these trips, but the effort was well worth the difficulties involved, as the countryside in the summer at this altitude was beautiful with, wild flowers of all kinds in bloom everywhere and clear streams cascading down the valleys

Plate 5

Winter scene of snow covered
Mountains of Lesotho

Expatriate officers were entitled to annual local leave and this gave us the opportunity to make several interesting trips into South Africa during our tour in Lesotho, and three of these I particularly remember. The first trip was to go south from Lesotho into that area of the Natal Province known as the Transkei, a beautiful part of South Africa that stretches down to the Indian Ocean and here we stayed in great luxury in a small hotel virtually on the beach. It must be said that the secondary roads through the Transkei were appalling at that time and for many miles we crashed and rattled over rough gravel surfaces that consisted of exposed oversize stone guaranteed to damage car shock absorbers if nothing else. Seldom have I been so glad to see the Indian Ocean and to know that we would not have to repeat this driving experience, for at least another fortnight!

We had travelled in convoy with a Swedish Engineer and his family who were good friends of ours from Lesotho. In their company, we had a very pleasant holiday, swimming in the sea or in a beautiful inland lagoon that adjoined the beach, playing bad golf on the hotel golf course among the sand dunes or tennis on the hotel hard courts. The food was excellent, crayfish, prawns and other sea fish made regular appearances on the menu and we were accommodated in well-furnished bungalows adjoining the beach. Altogether an idyllic holiday with good friends and companions, marred only by the thoughts of the dreadful road journey back to Lesotho!

Our next local leave involved a trip to the North East of Lesotho into the Drakensburg Mountains, a high mountain range along which ran along the border of

Lesotho with South Africa. Here we stayed in the mountain resort of Little Switzerland where accommodation was of the more conventional type in standard hotel rooms. The scenery was quite spectacular, mountains rising all around the high valley in which the resort was sited and the air was cool during the day and very cold at night, as might be expected at such a high altitude. It was inevitable, I suppose, that I would find some fishing for trout in the streams at this altitude!

My young son and myself found a small dam near the hotel that was reputed to be stocked with trout and evening found us hopefully fly fishing in this water. As far as I can recall, we both caught some small rainbow trout, but my main recollection of that expedition is the green snake, which suddenly appeared swimming in front of me. No matter where I moved along the dam, he persisted in following me, with his head up as if about to strike at any moment. I convinced myself that he was a harmless grass snake, but his continual presence in front of me as I cast out my fly did not improve my concentration on my fly and casting!

Our third expedition away from Lesotho was to stay with old friends from our Kenya days who had settled in Pietermaritzburg in the Natal Province of South Africa. This was in the days of apartheid in South Africa and we had our first taste of this when we arrived in the outskirts of Pietermaritzburg and stopped to ask our way to our friend's house. Our car was quickly surrounded by Asians who, I must say, tried to be most helpful, but pointed out that we were in that area of the town set aside for Asians so all they could do was to tell us how to reach the 'White' area. After several more enquiry stops, we finally found our friends house, by which time darkness had descended and we were very glad indeed to have finally reached our destination.

We spent a very pleasant weekend in our friends' very comfortable bungalow that had its own swimming pool and all modern conveniences – something that was sometimes lacking in Lesotho where power cuts were frequent and our furniture was basic Government Issue.

In Maseru, we were the proud owners of a Government Issue electric cooker that did not always work according to its scheduled switches! Very often, the grill switch turned on the oven and vice versa and sometimes both grill and oven came on together. After several trips to the Government Electrician's workshop which only resulted in it being returned with further complications, we decided to live with what we had and not tempt fate any further.

Anyway, to return to our weekend in Pietermaritzburg, we arrived on a Saturday and after an excellent early breakfast, our friends packed a picnic luncheon and we took off to the farm of a settler who had a dam stocked with rainbow trout. My friend and I waded in to do some fly-fishing before it became too hot. We had good sport and landed several nice rainbow trout, but by 11.30 a.m. all fish activity ceased as the heat of the day increased, so we rejoined our wives and retired to the shade of a nearby tree. Here we yarned of old times in East Africa and drank beer until it was time to have our picnic lunch. In the afternoon, we returned to the house and relaxed in their swimming pool. The following day we had to return to Lesotho and I must say we did envy the lifestyle of our friends who had made their new life in South Africa, where he had found a well-paid job.

Personally I think I would have found it very difficult to live in an apartheid system and I always thought that it could not last, which, of course, is what transpired in the end.

Road construction in Lesotho was, by now, being funded by several Aid Agencies and by the time we finished our second tour and finally left Lesotho, the road network was well advanced and maintenance systems in place and operational. One of the worst things about working abroad is that when you finally have to leave, you leave behind many new friends and colleagues of different races and colours. So it was with Lesotho. Some of these new friends you will meet again if you continue to work in the Aid Agency circle, but many you will never see again. Lesotho was I think, unique in the number of nationalities that were represented in the Ministry of Works during the time I was there. At one time, the Roads Branch had engineers from France, Britain, Sweden, Norway, U.S.A., India, Australia, Germany, Austria and Ireland all working together and generally speaking, they all got on very well with each other. As Deputy Chief Roads Engineer and therefore the Senior Expatriate Engineer in the Branch, (the Chief Roads Engineer was an extremely able and likeable Basotho) I had many dealings with the expatriate staff and my wife and I made good friends with the wives and families of many engineers of different nationalities.

CHAPTER 13.
TO SWAZILAND

During our time in Lesotho, we had visited Swaziland and Malawi on our local leaves, and we had been very impressed with what we had seen of Swaziland.

When I realised that British Aid was looking for a Senior Engineer to run the Roads Branch of the Swaziland Ministry of Works, I was not slow to apply for the post and after being duly interviewed in London, was offered the post on a two and one half year contract. So, once again, we packed our bags and returned to another part of Southern Africa.

Swaziland was also a small African Kingdom, which was situated to the North of the Republic of South Africa, and bounded by it on three sides, the fourth side being bounded by the country of Mozambique. The Swazi tribe had affiliations with the Zulus of South Africa, but differed from this warlike tribe in that they had never been conquered in battle by the European invaders, but had always settled their differences by negotiation, an historical circumstance of which they were extremely proud.

As a tribe, they were a very friendly people and appeared to have little of the prejudice against white people that does exist in some other African countries. Walking on a street in Mbabane (the Capital City of Swaziland) was like being in Ireland in some ways, as anyone who caught your eye would greet you in a friendly manner, something that was not likely to happen too often in Lesotho. The climate of Swaziland was very different to that of Lesotho as it was a good deal nearer the Equator and although a mountainous area, it had no really cold weather. In fact, it was extremely hot and unpleasantly humid in the summer in the lowland areas where sugar cane and cotton were the main cash crops.

A large section of the higher part of the country was planted with forestry and this was another major industry. Other areas grew oranges, lemons and bananas as cash crops and there was a steady trade with South Africa in all these items. All in all, a very different country to Lesotho, with a sound economy and a thriving tourist business with South Africans that gave employment in the many good hotels and restaurants which had been developed for this purpose in the environs of the capital city of Mbabane.

The country was a strong monarchy and had managed in a very unusual way to combine native customs with modern living. The King had great power and there were a great number of Princes and Princesses who were descended from the many wives of his father. At the time of our arrival in Swaziland, there was a Queen Regent, as the young man chosen to succeed as King was still at school in U.K. However, he was duly crowned King of Swaziland during our time in the country and we were lucky enough, as senior expatriate civil servants, to be invited to the Coronation celebration. It was a ceremony of great splendour that was held out of doors in the Mbabane Sports Stadium. The Coronation Ceremony proper had already been held in the Royal Kraal, in accordance with Swaziland custom.

The new King had vowed to continue the old customs as well as the new, as had been his father's tradition, so he was required to take several wives. By the time we were finally leaving the country five years later, he had already acquired several young wives. The young King had his modern palace and his traditional kraal and both were used according to the particular requirement of the time – modern or traditional. Swazis could marry or be buried either in church or by traditional ceremony or both. There were native Courts where Chiefs presided, and Legal Courts based on British Law. There was a Parliament building that operated on the same basis as the British House of Commons and an equivalent Council of Elders, which dealt with Traditional Law.

In Government Offices and the Parliament, civil servants dressed either in European or Traditional dress. Traditional dress consisted of a colourful toga type garment, which was draped to leave one shoulder bare, and on formal occasions, a spear and shield were carried. In Parliament (which I had to attend when the Minister had to answer questions on roads), it was obligatory to wear a tie. This only came to my attention when I brought the Roads Branch Financial Controller, who was an American, with me to answer some queries on the Roads Budget. He was told to go home and put on a tie. It transpired that he did not have a tie in his wardrobe in Swaziland, so I had to send him with a hasty note to my wife, asking her to outfit him with one of my ties!

Swaziland had a policy of keeping on good terms with all its neighbours and allowing Europeans to run a good deal of its commercial activities, so this meant, being adjacent to South Africa, that there was a great deal of South African influence in the country. This was an unusual situation at this time, as most independent African countries were totally opposed to South Africa because of the apartheid policies of the Government of that country. South Africa was also very interested in opening up trade with Mozambique and Swaziland bordered Mozambique, so there was great pressure on Swaziland to construct a good standard main road from the South African Border to the Mozambique Border.

This project became was one of the main road construction jobs that I had to contend with during my time in Swaziland. Unlike Lesotho, Swaziland had already a reasonable road network in existence when I took over as Chief Engineer of the Roads Branch and apart from the road mentioned above, my job was mainly to obtain funds to upgrade the existing network and design a viable maintenance system.

After the usual initial stay in a hotel in Mbabane, we were allocated a nice Government house in the suburbs of the City and settled in to the usual expatriate existence. We found there were two small Game Reserves near Mbabane and often visited these on weekends. They contained giraffe, wildebeest, zebra, warthog and various kinds of antelope and at the time we were there, there was an attempt being made to introduce white rhino as well. One of these Game Reserves, situated north of Mbabane, contained three small dams, which had, been stocked with rainbow trout, so it was not long before I had my fly rod out and had some nice fishing with the rainbow trout that thrived in these conditions. I had two interesting meetings with the local reserve inhabitants, both of which occurred as I was crossing the narrow path across the earth embankment of one of the dams.

On the first occasion, I met a very truculent Kudu bull with a fine set of the long sharp horns that go with his breed. He intended to cross the dam wall in the opposite direction to me and after a short confrontation; I gave him right of way. On the second occasion, I met a warthog sow followed by three young and this time I did not even wait to see what would happen!

Swaziland abounded with a tremendous variety of birds, many of which had beautiful colourings. I particularly remember the beautiful Malachite Kingfishers that so often were my companions when I fished in the dams. It was fascinating to watch them hovering over the dam and then diving suddenly into the water, reappearing almost immediately with a tiny fish in their beaks. They took little notice of me as I waded in the dam casting my flies near them. The reeds around the dams would be alive with small birds; particularly visible would be the incredible bishop bird, a tiny little bird resplendent in his bright red regalia. Weaverbirds and yellow canaries were also common and the egg-shaped hanging nests of weaverbirds were festooned in large numbers from available trees.

In our garden, an occasional visitor was the African Hoopoe, a beautifully marked bird with an orange and black crest. Not such popular visitors to the garden were the mousebirds, clever little birds that arrived in large flocks and could do great damage to any fruit or vegetables that you were growing. I once saw them in a bunch bouncing up and down on top of a fruit net in order to push it down far enough to reach the fruit below. An intelligent and destructive little bird. Mousebirds had the unusual habit of perching together in a tight close bunch and they would run up and down the branches and trunks of trees looking just like little mice – the reason, of course, why they were called mouse birds.

The climate of Swaziland, being a good deal more tropical than Lesotho, produced warmer evenings. As a result it was more feasible to sit out in the evenings and enjoy the luxury of barbecues and drinks parties in the open air most of the year – something which the more extreme climate of Lesotho limited to summer evenings only. It must be said, however, that it also rained a good deal more in Swaziland and some evenings would be spent sitting on the veranda, swotting the numerous large flying insects and being nearly deafened by the cacophony of frogs in the valley below as they went through their mating antics

Another of the great assets of Swaziland, resulting at least partly from its Tourist Industry, was the great variety of restaurants available in Mbabane and its environs. They varied from an interesting Portuguese one, famous for its sardines and prawns and its ferocious piri-piri sauce, to excellent Italian and Swiss restaurants, a genuine German one producing good German staple foods like Weiner Schnitzel and Beef with good solid dumplings, and the inevitable Chinese restaurant (but a good one!). Add to these the restaurants of several hotels and you have a regular gourmet's paradise! Unfortunately, pressure of work and a Senior Engineer's salary did not permit us to become involved in all the eating out possibilities of

Swaziland, which was probably just as well for the sake of our health.

I know many people who have never been involved in working in Third World countries believe that we, who work in these Countries as expatriates, have a great life style and have little to do, but it has certainly not been my experience. The pressure of work in my job was such that I seldom was able to leave my office until long after the local civil servants had gone home and there were few Saturday mornings and many Sunday afternoons that I had to go into the office to clear my desk for the following week. Having said that, it was true, of course, that one had servants and the best of facilities in a good climate, at least, as far as Swaziland was concerned.

At the end of our first year in Swaziland, we became due for some local leave and we flew down to Cape Town in South Africa for a few days change of scenery. This was our second visit to this area, as we had landed there for a short visit on retiring from Kenya, when we had opted to go home via the Cape by ship. On that occasion we had arrived in mid-winter and been greeted by snow showers and very cold windy weather. One tends to forget that Cape Town is nearly as far South of the Equator as the British Isles are North of it, so it has a very definite summer and winter and the winter, I understand, can be fairly unpleasant at times.

It was autumn when we arrived at the Cape and the weather was reasonably warm, but, as I recall, it drizzled rain on our first day. We hired a car and did all the usual tourist things. We drove out to Cape Point where one looked out to the sea at the Cape of Good

Hope and here there was an interesting small Nature Reserve where the famous protea plants grew and many types of unusual heathers and other flowering plants. We visited Stellenbosch, sampled the wine in various vineyards, and admired the Old Dutch architecture of the buildings in this area. We walked the sea front of Cape Town and enjoyed excellent South African cuisine in some of the many restaurants. For the first time I saw the small Cape Coloured people – to me they seemed very similar to pictures one sees of the Bushmen of the Kalahari Desert, but they were much lighter in colour and said to be descended from the original Hottentot people of the Cape. We found the inhabitants of the Cape friendly and helpful and were quite sorry to have to return to Swaziland.

At the end of our first thirty-month tour in Swaziland, I was asked to come back for a second tour and agreed to do this, as I anticipated retiring to Ireland at the end of this time.

At the time of our return to Swaziland, several young Swazis were completing their engineering degree courses in various overseas countries and returning to work in their home country. It was now part of my job to ensure that those young graduates, some of whom were posted to the Roads Branch of the Ministry of Works, rapidly gained the necessary experience to take over the Engineer posts in the Branch from the expatriate engineers, who were being funded by various AID Agencies.

This I set out to do by posting them initially to Construction Units in the field, where they would gain essential practical experience, before being attached as Assistants to the expatriate Section Heads of the Branch.

In the main, I think that this proved a very successful operation, but there were, inevitably I suppose, one or two of these young men who felt they knew it all and resented not being able to walk straight into a Senior Engineer Post.

Anyway, by the time I completed my second tour in Swaziland, the demand for the few qualified African Engineers, both in local Consultancies and South Africa had become so great, that, inevitably, the attraction of higher salaries lured away some of the newly qualified Roads staff. As a result, the Government had to request AID Agencies once again to fill some of these posts with Expatriate staff, until more Swazi graduates became available.

For our last local leave in Swaziland, we took a plane trip to Malawi and travelled around that country for a few days. We were very impressed with the Malawian people that we saw and met on this trip. The Country is long and comparatively narrow in shape and encompasses half of Lake Nyasa that runs for most of its length. It bounds Mozambique on the East, Zambia on the West and Tanzania on the North, so it has no sea access and must depend for this on the goodwill of its neighbours.

At the time when we visited, the country was poor and kept its imports to a minimum, which encouraged local industries to produce many of the goods that were imported from South Africa, Kenya and Europe in many other Southern African Countries. Poor they were, but they appeared to be a very happy, honest and hardworking people and petty crime was low and the police respected, something that was not very obvious in some other African countries.

We hired a car in the Capital City, Lilongwe, and duly booked in to a hotel for the night. Lilongwe was an eye-opener to us. It is not often that one sees a Capital City that has been "purpose-built"- Lilongwe was such a place and it seemed to us that it had been remarkably well designed for this purpose. Commercial buildings and Government Offices were built in surroundings of native woods and shrubs and kept well apart from each other, with minimal building heights allowed. The result was a very beautiful City in most pleasant surroundings. The drawback for visitors was the difficulty of finding places such as Banks and Garages, so well were they hidden in the scenery!

The day after our arrival, we explored Lilongwe and, incidentally, returned the hired car to its owners for exchange to a more reliable model. It had become obvious that the vehicle we had been given would not have travelled far on the roads of Malawi without serious problems. We then set off North to stay in the Elephant Game Park that had been recommended by the Tourist Board. It soon became obvious to us that the roads of Malawi were suffering from lack of finance for re-construction purposes. Speaking as a Roads Engineer, I have never seen worn out road pavements patched to such an extent. For many miles we travelled on a complete patchwork quilt of tarmac, beautifully patched in perfect squares and rectangles in the most admirable fashion – but there was virtually none of the original road surface left between the patches! One could only presume that funds were not available to do anything else. I wish I could have persuaded some of my own Road Engineers to carry out pavement patching to such a standard.

Anyway we duly arrived at the gates of the Game Reserve and drove slowly and carefully along the gravel-surfaced road in pouring rain and eventually reached the Camp just as dusk was falling, having had to stop for a herd of elephant to cross the road on our way. We were allocated a 'Rondavel' type bedroom i.e. a circular thatched building based on the traditional African hut – a cool and comfortable type of construction for this climate. Our room looked out on a man-made dam where, as we watched two elephant came down to drink, one of which was a large bull wearing an electronic collar.

After a shower and the usual sundowner drink, we had an excellent meal and retired for the night. The following day we drove around the Park's narrow dirt roads and saw numerous herds of elephant. In fact there were really too many of them and they came too close for comfort, as they could appear suddenly in front of you on the road out of the thick bush on each side with little warning! That afternoon, we were sitting at the entrance of our Rondavel, when the bull elephant with the collar attached strolled into the camp. Our accommodation was the second building in from the camp perimeter and we watched, with some anxiety, while the bull wandered up to the first Rondavel. A young couple with a baby, whom we had met and spoken with earlier, occupied this room. They had left their baby, asleep in its pram, on the veranda of their room, whilst they went down to the dam and walked out on the small jetty to admire the view. Whilst we watched, in the bull moved to the entrance of their Rondavel and with his trunk lifted the mosquito net off the baby's pram, and inspected the occupant!

Apparently satisfied with his inspection, he then replaced the net cover and ambled over to our accommodation.

Hurriedly we retreated off our veranda and back into the main room of the Rondavel, only to see, with horror, an enormous head filling the door opening! There followed an inquisitive trunk that snuffled its way around the interior of the room, whilst we shrank against the back wall. Apparently deciding that there was nothing more he wanted to know about our belongings, or us, the head withdrew and the bull elephant continued on his tour of he camp. In fact, he stayed around the camp for quite some time and before he finally departed, he scared the daylights out of an Italian family, who evidently thought it would be fun to have their photograph taken standing in front of him. Being Italians, they could not accomplish this without a great deal of shouting and gesticulating. The bull elephant's reaction to this was to make a false charge at them, which changed their minds swiftly.

I spoke to the African Game Scout in the camp about this episode and enquired if he thought it was safe to allow this bull elephant (whose name apparently was 'Bill') to wander around inside the camp like this. He said that so far, this Bill had caused no problems, but the last two, (apparently also named Bill) had had to be shot because they became too troublesome!

I think we were quite relieved that our stay ended after the second night and we wended our way back South towards the City of Blantyre. This was Christmas day and we had booked into a hotel on the shore of Lake Nyasa, and were looking forward to a nice Christmas Dinner that night. We arrived on a very hot evening with the sun going down over the lake and producing a blinding heat into the room we were allocated.

It was at this stage that we discovered there was no air-conditioning in our room, only a small and totally inadequate wall fan. Our next discovery was that the Hotel had had a Christmas luncheon party for the staff and their children and there was to be no Christmas dinner for us! Anyway, we settled for the only available alternative, which was the tilapia fish from Lake Nyasa and I must admit, that it is an exceptionally good fish to eat. We got little sleep that night in the heavy, humid heat and the next day drove south to Blantyre.

I do not recall very much about Blantyre, except that it seemed to be a pleasant town with good shops, where we made some purchases and spent a night in a good hotel. Having been assured by the Tourist Office that trout fishing, together with the necessary tackle, was available on the Zomba Plateau, we booked in a hotel there and drove up the following day. When I say drove "up" to the Zomba Plateau, I am not exaggerating, as the road went up the hills in a series of narrow hairpin bends that gave frightening views of the land below as we crawled round the steep turns. Finally, we arrived at the hotel on the top and since our stay was for only one night, I enquired about the trout fishing as soon as we had moved into our room.

It was then that the fun started. It transpired that the hotel was the proud owner of three decrepit fly rods, one fly reel with about ten feet of nylon attached and no flies or other baits. The Management then informed me that they thought I could get nylon and flies in the village at the base of the escarpment. So I set forth once again down the terrifying escarpment road, found the village shop concerned and - guess what! The Indian owner had no nylon or flies! Back I drove again up to the hotel, to be informed that the Game Scout in charge of the fishing was known to have fly fishing equipment. Off I set again to the Game Camp, which, at any rate, was not far away and finally located, the Scout. This man had a fly rod with a broken tip tied together with string and a reel with a slightly longer piece of nylon, but only one fly. All this he was prepared to rent to me at an exorbitant price. Anyway, we struck a bargain and I went fishing and lost 'the fly' in the first hour, so that concluded my fishing expedition in Malawi.

We drove back to Lilongwe, returned our battered hired car and caught the plane back to Swaziland. An interesting holiday, which, I think, we both enjoyed in spite of its rather scary moments.

CHAPTER 14
THE WORST OF AFRICA

Our tour in Swaziland ended and once again, we returned to Ireland. This time I had made it clear to my contacts that I would only go abroad again on short-term consultancies as I felt the time to retire was close at hand.

So it was, that one night, I was awoken at 2 a.m. by the ringing of the phone in our bedroom. On answering, a cheerful American voice asked me if I would go out to West Africa for them on a Consultancy to sort out some World Bank funded contracts that were in trouble. The caller sounded very surprised that it was still the middle of the night in Ireland. I said I might consider it if I received all the details and in due course these arrived.

I had never been in West Africa and the temptation was too much for me, despite the horror stories I had been told by friends who had been in those parts in times gone by. For reasons that will become obvious as the story of this stay in West Africa proceeds, I do not intend to name the country to which I had committed myself for this consultancy.

It was some weeks later that I stood, in a milling mass of Africans with a scattering of Europeans, sweltering in high humidity in the arrivals hall of an Airport, and began to wonder if I had been completely mad to undertake this assignment. The passengers crowding around the exits did not attempt to form orderly queues, but pushed and jostled in a heaving mass waving their passports at the Military Officers standing around the exit. I had forgotten, until then, that this country was under military rule and I now saw that an Army Officer stood beside every official trying to deal with the mob.

I was relieved to hear my name being called and made contact with a well-dressed African who said he was from one of the local Civil Engineering Consultancy and had been asked to meet me and help with the red tape. He then introduced me to another local who, he said, was there to assist us through the system. I subsequently was informed that this gentleman was, in fact, an employee of the Customs Department! With considerable relief, I followed my new colleague as he forced his way to the windows of the Immigration Officials. I was surprised to see that these windows were fitted with one-way glass, so the officials could see me, but I could not see them. As directed by my new acquaintance I pushed my passport under the glass panel and our guide disappeared behind the desk to talk with the unseen officials. There are few things as soul-destroying as standing in front of a one-way glass window through which you can see nothing, but knowing that you are being observed from the other side. Our friend finally reappeared as my passport came back under the glass above the counter. The Passport had not been stamped and I was told by my associate to return it again with a sterling five-pound note enclosed. I did as I was told and it reappeared after a very short time duly endorsed with a three-month stay visa.

We then joined another mob that was trying to clear their baggage and leave the Airport via a customs inspection table where there stood two Customs officers flanked by two military officers. Despite vociferous objections from other unfortunate passengers, my guide fought his way, with us in attendance, to the Customs Table, where I was told to place my luggage on the table and open all my bags. Once again, our new friend came into action and went behind the counter clutching one of my five pound notes and spoke to the officials. I was then angrily waved on by one of the military officers and was able to close up my cases.

Finally, we reached daylight and entered the sticky heat of the Airport car park, where, after my colleague had settled up with our guide, we embarked in an air-conditioned Mercedes car and entered the traffic stream. The traffic moved at great speed and no one gave way to anyone else if at all possible. Entering a traffic junction or an island required great nerve and was accompanied by much shouting and horn blowing on both sides. It was necessary to exit a junction at great speed in order to mesh in with the fast moving main traffic stream. Never had I seen such incredible driving in the past and I watched with a mixture of admiration and terror as we wended our way through a maze of traffic to finally reach a very comfortable hotel where I was to spend my first night in West Africa.

Very few Expatriates could be seen driving themselves, probably because they lacked the necessary nerve! I was to find out later that any local, who had the least pretensions to be important, possessed at least one car and driver for himself and another for his wife! As one might expect, this reckless driving was responsible for the numerous accidents that I was later to see as I moved around the country.

My local colleague informed me that it would be necessary to take another plane the following morning, in order to reach the town where I would be based to carry out the Consultancy Project. This small town was apparently some 400 miles to the southeast of the capital city. It was nearly 11 a.m. by the time he reappeared on the following morning and by the time we reached the domestic terminal of the national airline, the 'plane we were meant to board had already left. This development caused considerable surprise to my African colleague, who clearly had not expected the 'plane in question to leave within some hours of its scheduled timetable, and I got the impression that he felt the airline had taken somewhat of a liberty in leaving only three quarters of an hour later than the timetable indicated!

Anyway, we now drove to another airfield, which was apparently, the home base of a privately operated airline and here we were informed that a plane to our destination was due to leave within an hour. We sat and sweltered for two and one half hours, in what must have been originally and old air force base building- a corrugated iron structure with no air conditioning and few fans. Seldom have I been so hot, sticky, and full of regret that I ever got involved in this project.

Finally a 'plane arrived, taxied up to the entrance of the terminal and started to discharge its load of passengers. At this stage my colleague had hired an airline employee to assist us on to the 'plane and he now came rushing up and said we must queue outside in the open whilst the remainder of the passengers disembarked. Whilst we were doing this, he disappeared on to the 'plane and came back to say that he had arranged seats for us and he would now take our place in the queue, whilst we stood in the shade under the wing of the 'plane. By now, I was no longer surprised at anything which could happen, so we stood like royalty under the shelter of the wing of the 'plane while he stood in the queue on our behalf.

When our employee finally reached the boarding steps, he went on board with our hand baggage, then came back, and held back the queue whilst we boarded. After this, he showed us to our seats and departed. Perhaps the most astonishing part of this episode was the fact that none of the other passengers, queuing all this time in the blazing sun, remonstrated with him or us about this carry-on, so one can only assume that it was quite a regular occurrence.

It was only when the 'plane was well on its way and I had time to look around me, that I realised from the literature and furnishings that I was on one of the old Aer Lingus 'planes which used to fly from Dublin to London. Not unnaturally I began to wonder whether this old 'plane was being properly maintained and serviced by this private air line, but in spite of my premonitions, it duly arrived safely at its destination. It then transpired that this was my African colleague's base, but that I had a further fifty miles of road travel in front of me and the transport had not yet arrived. There then took place a series of abortive telephone calls on a system that clearly did not operate too well, and eventually, I was taken to a small hotel to spend another night on my journey.

I arrived at the hotel just as the electricity failed and I was condemned to the misery of trying to sleep without air conditioning after a cold candlelit supper of tough ham and tinned fruit. Early the next morning, my transport arrived and I finally reached the offices of the main U.S.A. Consultants with whom I was to work for the next six weeks.

The Project Director of the Consultancy was a very likeable flamboyant American whose trademark was apparently a large cigar, which stayed, seldom lit, but nearly always in place, in the side of his mouth. I must say that we got on very well together and he and his wife were extremely kind to me during my stay, and always made me welcome in their house and looked after me during the weekends, which can be very lonely on these short consultancy projects. I recall two hilarious golf games that we played on weekends on the local golf course. On each occasion, we had the golf course to ourselves, so we had the pick of numerous caddies. The course obviously did not see a mower very often and it was quite difficult to find the 'greens'- (they were in fact sand surfaced and required brushing each time we used them) in the long grass and abundant vegetation. Without a local caddy, I doubt if we could have found our way around the course at all! It all made for hilarious golf and suited us as neither of us were great golfers. Only by despatching the caddy down the fairway to mark the line was it possible to ascertain where the next hole was sited. We lost plenty of golf balls but we had fun. Some Portuguese consultants came round on another evening and we played poker for minor stakes. They were very pleasant company, as I was to experience again in all my subsequent dealings with Portuguese nationals.

I was accommodated in an excellent, recently built hotel, which was equipped to deal with the vagaries of the mains electricity, since it had been fitted with stand-by generators. Electricity supply was a constant problem during my stay in this country. It might come on for two or three hours in the morning and then be off for the rest of the day, or possibly come on again for an hour or two in the evening. After one horrific experience in a lift when electric failed whilst between floors and I was alone without light or air-conditioning for over an hour, I refused to use the lifts and went up and down the stairs in all premises that had lifts installed.

Even after I came home, I was very unhappy in travelling in lifts for some considerable time following this experience. It is one thing to have a lift failure when you know that ringing the alarm system will bring assistance, but in parts of Africa, it might be many hours or even days before anyone who understands the mechanism becomes available.

The food was not great, meat was scarce and tough, chickens scrawny and of poor quality and bacon very fat and greasy. I have to say that the staff were excellent, pleasant and helpful in every way and it came as an unpleasant shock to me to come back from work one day and find the staff all out on strike and the hotel closed. It transpired that they had not been paid for some weeks and, not unnaturally, were not prepared to carry on. Sadly, I packed my belongings and moved to another smaller and not so pleasant hotel, where they had no standby electric generators!

I was given the use of an office in the Ministry of Works and the American Consultants supplied a vehicle and excellent driver who was able to infiltrate the awful traffic without scaring me too much. With the assistance of two local professionals, I was eventually able to disentangle the mess of unfinished contracts and find the reason for their non-completion was simple. The contractors had not been paid, so they left the job!

As to why they had not been paid, when they had submitted invoices and Aid funds were theoretically available I did not enquire further. I merely listed what was owing to them and reported this back to the World Bank. When my report was ready to write, it transpired that the Ministry Offices had plenty of typists, but only electric typewriters and no electricity most days after 11a.m! I sent for my invaluable driver to scour the town and try to hire a manual typewriter, but it seemed that only one small and rather ancient typewriter could be found and on this the basics of my report was laboriously typed.

My consultancy time in West Africa had now expired, so I packed my bags and said I would complete the report at home and send it directly to the World Bank. I was then informed by the Chief Engineer that the Minister wanted to see the report before I left. I had visions at this stage of being forced to re-write the report or being indefinitely detained in the country, so I sent for my ever reliable driver and we drove back to the Capital and I booked on a flight for the following day.

For the first time I was on my own at the Airport. I duly arrived at the required two hours before departure to join a long queue at the ticket counter. Again, there was a military officer at the Ticket counter, the Security section and the Emigration counter. I stood in the first queue for a long time and then noticed that people were being called out of the queue to the desk out of turn. There was a European standing behind me who I had been chatting to, he apparently worked in an Oil Company, and so I asked him what was happening.

He said, "Have you not got some local assisting you?"

I admitted that I had not and he went on to say that in that case I might be there for a very long time. I then realised that each person being called out had a local who approached the Army Officer and spoke to him, after which in a short time their name was called and they left the queue and went through the system.

I pondered what to do and then decided to make my move. I marched up to the Officer, produced my identity letter from the World Bank, and waved it in front of him.

He glanced at it and said, "What is this all about". I suspected he could not read or understand the letter, so I said, "This is my authority from the World Bank to come here and carry out a Consultancy. This work is complete and I now need to return home urgently".

With an irritable wave of the hand, he told the ticket clerk to clear my baggage and I saw my two suitcases safely (as I thought!) on their way to the baggage handlers. I then proceeded to the next stop, which was the security desk with the usual arch to pass through. My experience of these machines had been that they usually sounded off if I did not take my small calculator and bunch of keys from my pocket and pass them to the Security men before going through the arch. I did this and went through, but without success, the machine pinged and the Security boys moved in on me. Somewhat mystified, I stood to be frisked, and at their request, I emptied all available metal items from my pockets. They showed little interest in these, but demanded to see my wallet. I assured them that I had no metal items in my wallet, but they insisted, so I took it out and opened it up.

It was then that I realised what was happening, as the contents were examined and one of them remarked "Eh! But you have a lot of English money in your wallet!"

So, I parted with another five-pound sterling note and was waved on my way once more, this time to the departure lounge where I felt at last that I had escaped from the system. I concluded later, that the setting on the security arch had probably been fixed so that it went off automatically every time anyone passed through it, whether they had metal objects in their pockets or not. By this means, the staff could get to see into all travellers' wallets and or purses and collect a nice little bonus, but perhaps I was being too suspicious!

But I was not out of the woods yet. Over the Tannoy came the message "Will Mr Barry please return to the ticket desk and clear his baggage." I had cleared my baggage and had my half of the baggage labels attached to my boarding pass to prove it, so there was no way I was going to return to the ticket desk and I remained in my seat. Some time later, an Army Officer appeared in the departure lounge and called my name. I answered and he said I must return with him to the ticket counter. I said I would not, and showed him my baggage labels, saying that my baggage was cleared and should by now be on the 'plane. He finally left and I really thought that this was the end of this extraordinary carry on, but I was to be mistaken.

When our flight was eventually called, we had once again to pass through a barrier, this time it was manned by a policewoman, and she demanded some money, so I had to part with another five pound sterling note before finally boarding the 'plane. So ended my time in this West African country, but when I arrived home - guess what! My baggage was missing!

I sent off a telegram to the Irish Consul and some days later my suitcases arrived in one piece. I must say, at this point, that in all my working time in Africa, I always found the various Irish Consuls in the territories where I worked, to be most helpful and friendly persons and a credit to their country.

After my experiences in West Africa, I vowed never again to make the mistake of going to this part of the Continent, and kept to this vow. When, subsequently, I was asked to do another short term Consultancy in this part of the world, I must admit the fee on offer tempted me. On reflection, however I realised that no money can pay for the personal danger one can get into in these countries, where military regimes are in control and corruption is rife, so I turned down this offer.

CHAPTER 15.
THE BEAUTIFUL PACIFIC

Two further short term Consultancies came my way, both involving a return to my old favourite country of Swaziland and then, out of the blue, I was asked if I would undertake a short term Consultancy in the Solomon Islands, which are situated in the Pacific, North East of Australia and East of New Guinea.

This, I felt would be a fitting end to my overseas career, as I had always wanted to visit this part of the world and I had a friend who had been Director of Public Works in the Solomon Islands and he had loved working there. Furthermore, I had a sister who had emigrated with her husband to Brisbane in Australia and this was one of the departure points for the Solomon Islands.

So, some weeks later, I found myself, after a long and very tiresome air flight, at Brisbane Airport, being greeted by my sister and husband. After a good night's sleep and a day to recover I was back at the Airport boarding a 'plane bound for the Solomon Islands. It was a wonderful daytime flight. In the clear blue Pacific below us I could see coral reefs and little islands scattered everywhere below us and for once I was quite sorry when we starting losing height to land in the Airport at Honiara on Guadalcanal Island, which was the Capital of the Solomon Islands.

We disembarked and walked into the small Airport building and waited while our luggage was unloaded by hand and brought into the Customs section of the building. Here the Customs officers made a cursory inspection of everyone's baggage. I was only asked one question – "Do you have any videos with you?"- I had not and would never have thought of bringing any. Apparently, the Government of the Islands was trying hard to prevent 'Adult' (i.e. pornographic) films coming into the country and I would certainly hope that they continue to be successful in this objective.

As I passed through Immigration, I beheld, to my astonishment, an old friend and engineer colleague from Lesotho, together with his wife, waiting to greet me. For me, this was a wonderful surprise, as it transpired that, not only was he working with the main Consultants for the project, but also he was the Team Leader of the Project. No one in the main Consultants Office in U.K. had told me he was here in this capacity and it meant that I was immediately working with a friend and colleague.

I was duly installed in a very pleasant hotel situated on the beach and Japanese owned. The climate for me was reminiscent of my days in Mombasa on the Kenya Coast. It was hot and sticky and it rained nearly every evening, a warm heavy tropical rain that did little to cool the air. The Hotel was air-conditioned, which at least allowed one to get a good night's rest, but when you went to the office it was like passing through a Turkish bath and you had only fans in the Ministry of Works Offices to try and keep reasonably cool during the day.

The inhabitants of Honiara, who represented people from many of the islands, which formed the Solomon Islands, were among the most friendly and helpful I have ever met on my travels. They were also the most laid back, and getting things done required great patience and perseverance!

The island of Guadalcanal was like most, if not all, of the islands, of volcanic origin and the high central area was covered in rain forest and very sparsely inhabited. The population were mostly of Melanesian extraction and were darker in colour than their Polynesian neighbours from islands further to the West.

I suppose one of the things that a stranger, like myself, coming to the islands would notice at once, was the large number of churches dotted around Honiara. There appeared to be many religious sects involved that were certainly new to me, but Christianity clearly paid a large part in the lives of the inhabitants.

Earth tremors were common and in fact, I experienced two in the short time that I was on the island. Traditional buildings and many of those rented by expatriates were built on stilts to allow for earth tremors and I can vouch for the fact that they could sway in the most alarming fashion on these occasions!

The local population lived in thatched buildings consisting of a more or less open platform built on stilts and these were obviously very suitable for the climatic conditions as they allowed free air circulation. Coconut plantations grew down to the beach along the shoreline and all kinds of tropical fruit, vegetables and root crops flourished in the hot, moist climate along the coastal strip. Fish of all shapes and sizes swam around the shore and I believe there was a thriving export business in fish to Australia and New Zealand.

European foods were imported in small quantities by ship and the arrival of one of the ships carrying these resulted in a rush of expatriates and locals to the supermarkets to buy what was available before stocks ran out again. Once a week there was an open market and this was a wonderfully colourful affair that was attended by most expatriates. On sale would be a great selection of tropical fruit and vegetables and it was a pleasure to be able to go around the stalls in peace and not be hassled, or in fear of pickpockets, as so often was the case in other developing countries.

It was on these occasions, that you realised what a variation there was in the genes of the population, though most of the population were very dark-skinned, there was a proportion of very handsome lighter skinned people and what I found most amazing, a selection of dark-skinned people with very blond hair. Locals told me that most of these blond headed inhabitants were from the neighbouring island of Malaita and I presume this was correct, but the origin of this unusual combination of colourings greatly intrigued me, as they did not appear to show any of the signs of part European descent which one might expect from this combination of colourings.

I have already said that the general population could be described as well 'laid back' and this easygoing culture was immediately noticeable in the Government Offices where we had been given accommodation for the project. Shorts and Hawaiian shirts in bright patterns and colours were common and runners were the standard footwear, though bare feet were also in evidence.

All this was a considerable and pleasant change from the formality required in most African countries where I have worked - here most African senior staff wore smart suits to the office and we expatriates were expected to wear long trousers and shirts with ties and sports coats in what was often uncomfortably hot weather.

My part of the project in the Solomon Islands was to re-draft and update the Roads Act. It certainly required re-drafting as I soon found out. The existing legislation had never been changed since the Country ceased to be a British Colony and, in consequence, many of the powers in the Act were still vested in the Governor of the Colony – a post that had, naturally, disappeared when the Country gained its Independence. Anyway, I spent a few weeks working on this project and duly reached the stage of completing a draft for a new Act. This now required detailed checking by the legal draughtsman and the Permanent Secretary and Minister, so, since things did not move very fast in that part of the world, it was decided that the best thing I could do was to go home and come back in a month's time to make any alterations necessary for a final draft.

This time I flew home via Papua, New Guinea and we landed at the airport near Port Moresby. Again, this flight was a wonderful experience for me, as we flew across a different section of the South Pacific Ocean and had tremendous views of the little islands and circular coral reefs that abounded in this area.

Whilst walking on the beach in Guadalcanal, amongst the coconut plantations, I had seen, floating in the sea, numerous coconuts that had fallen from the trees and been blown off the shore. I was amazed to see that some of these nuts had sprouted new shoots and marvelled how they could start to grow like this while floating in salt water.

Plate 6

Typical Local House in the
Solomon Islands

Plate 7

Some of the lovely children
of the Solomon Islanders

Plate 8

Market day in Honiara the
Capital City of the Solomon Islands

Now looking down from the 'plane in the clear blue sky, I saw several tiny islands below, surrounded by coral reefs and in the middle of some of these islands was a single coconut palm. Clearly, these palms had grown from nuts that had floated up on the coral reef when the islands were being formed and had rooted themselves in this fashion. I thought that this was an amazing feat of nature and showed how these little islands could develop vegetation.

I will never forget the landing at Port Moresby airport! The airport was situated in a valley between high mountains and at times the wings of the 'plane seemed to be nearly touching the sides of the mountains, but we set down safely. I would have liked to have spent some time in Papua, New Guinea, but we were only allowed to stay around the airport until our onward 'plane arrived and we took off for Singapore, where I spent a night before boarding the next 'plane for the long and tiresome journey to London and thence to Cork.

After a month at home, I was on a 'plane again for the long journey back to the Solomon Islands. On this occasion, I brought my wife with me (at my expense may I add!) as we intended to stop off in Australia with my sister for a few days on our return journey. We were allocated a flat in Honiara that, unfortunately, had an inadequate air- conditioning system, so we both found it very difficult to sleep at night, but we managed to explore a little more of the Island during weekends.

Guadalcanal had seen some major battles at sea and on the land between the Japanese and the Americans during World War II, and the remains of tanks and landing craft were still to be seen in some places. The sea area off Honiara was apparently called Iron Bottom Bay, because of the large number of wrecked warships, of both sides that had been sunk in the area. These wrecks provided excellent cover and feeding sites for the local fish population and as a result, there were a growing number of Australian tourists that came to dive in and around these wrecks. This provided some useful tourism income for the Solomon Islands.

We visited the fish market where there was an abundance of good eating fish to be purchased, in particular the strange parrot fish whose parrot- like beak was used for breaking off lumps of coral and this fish had firm white flesh which provided excellent eating. The Market also sold excellent tropical fruit of all kinds and a limited variety of fresh vegetables.

We ate out in various restaurants – one could get Japanese food in the Hotel and genuine Chinese food in other restaurants. There was a large Chinese population who ran many businesses and they had their own little China Town area.

We hired a small Mazda car, since the Government pickup vehicle that I was issued with had to be returned to the Government vehicle pool during the weekend, and made expeditions along the Coast. The road system of Honiara was not exactly extensive! Apart from the internal road system of the city, which served the residential and small industrial areas, there were only two main roads. One ran East and West along the shoreline, with Honiara situated somewhere near the middle of it. The other did the same on the opposite side of the Island, but they did not meet each other!

In the circumstances, we were confined to the road out of Honiara and drove out on this in both directions on several occasions. The road had apparently been built by the Americans during the war and had seen better days. Trips to the East of Honiara required negotiating enormous potholes in which a vehicle could almost completely disappear, and deviations had to be made into the adjoining farmland on occasion. Road maintenance did not appear to be much in evidence!

Some miles to the west there was a small restaurant situated on the beach and we visited here on a couple of occasions and went swimming in the incredibly warm waters of the Pacific. It was here, on one visit that a shoal of small fish came in near to the shore and we were treated to a show of hungry skua birds crashing into the sea and gorging themselves on the baitfishes. This was the first time that I recall having seen skuas close up and they were an impressive sight – nearly pitch black in colour and with very long forked tails and very sharp looking beaks.

I was amazed at the way that everyone, local and expatriate, bathed and swam happily in these waters which must surely have been full of sharks, but perhaps the sheer quantity of fish food available meant that the shark population did not bother coming in close to the shore.

Walking on paths through the coconut plantations had their own hazards as coconuts were continually falling all around you. Everywhere you went the locals smiled and waved at you and they had no objection to you photographing them or their unique houses, a practice that in Africa would be tolerated only if some money was forthcoming.

As regards the Project, I found on my return that neither the Ministry Officials nor the Legal Draughtsman appeared to have read my draft of the Roads Act, so I set myself the task of writing draft standard letters which could be used by the road engineers to deal with infringements and other matters under the revised Act. This was done assuming, of course, that it was ever enacted!

This work complete, my wife and I returned to Australia and started our short holiday in that country. We stayed for the first few days with my sister and brother-in-law in Brisbane. At that time of the year, the weather was hot, but not too unpleasant and we saw the sights, met their neighbours, and had a pleasant stay.

We then flew down to stay with Irish friends who had settled in Tasmania. This was a total change from Brisbane. Hobart, the capital city of Tasmania, had apparently been one of the ports where the convicts from Britain had been sent in the early days. It was a fascinating place, buildings in the old port area seemed to me to be much more typical of a port in the U.K. than anything we had seen in other parts of Australia.

The vegetation and scenery of the surrounding area was more like our British Isles than a tropical climate. Those friendly people we met were obviously proud of being in Tasmania and by the time we left, I felt that if I had to live in Australia, this is where I would prefer to settle. Perhaps my ideas were influenced by the knowledge that this part of Australia was also renowned for its excellent trout fishing!

So, once again, we boarded a 'plane to return home to Ireland. For the third time I landed at Singapore and this time my wife and I had some time to do a bit of exploring in this City, before we left on that long and tiresome journey back to London.

We did not have time to visit the old city and markets of Singapore, but we did have time to look around the new shopping area and have tea in the famous Raffles Hotel. The new Singapore is a clean and handsome city, but it seemed to us to have little of the character, which one would expect, from a city in the Far East.

Everything was up to date and worked and the standard of cleanliness was only incredible to those of us who are used to the rather poor standards of Ireland. The floors in the Airport were spotless and there were little Chinese to be seen everywhere cleaning and polishing. In fact, one felt that as you walked along the enormous marbled floored halls that there was a little man behind you polishing off your footprints! Even on the numerous escalators there were cleaners going up and down polishing the handrails behind you.

After a good night's sleep in an excellent hotel we boarded our flight back to London, thence to Ireland and back to the reality that this time I had really retired.

So, I complete this account of my days as an overseas civil engineer. I consider that I have been very lucky to have seen and done so much in one short lifetime and even more lucky to have had a wife and family who have always put up with me and the often difficult times that go with working in developing countries.

We can look back on the many interesting times we have had and the friends of many different nationalities and creeds we have made in several developing countries over the years. I am glad to say that we are still in contact with many of these friends and those that are still living in far-away places continue to turn up at our door every now and again.